MORE THAN WORDS

DANNY NINAL

MORE THAN WORDS

CONTENTS

Dedication
viii

— INTRODUCTION
1

— MESSAGE FROM THE AUTHOR
2

— Text Insert
0

— HOW TO USE THIS BOOK
4

1 — THE FEEDING OF THE FIVE THOUSAND
7

2 — THE STORY OF ABIGAIL
13

3 — THE STORY OF THE BOY JESUS
17

4 — THE STORY OF THE CANAANITE WOMAN
21

5 — THE STORY OF THE DAUGHTERS OF ZELOPHEHAD
25

6 — THE STORY OF DEBORAH
31

7 — THE STORY OF ELIZABETH
35

8 — THE STORY OF ESTHER
39

9 — THE STORY OF HAGAR
45

10 — THE STORY OF HANNAH
49

11 — THE STORY OF JACOB & ESAU
55

12 — THE STORY OF JETHRO & MOSES
59

13 — THE STORY OF JOHN THE BAPTIST
63

14 — THE STORY OF JONATHAN
67

15 — THE STORY OF JOSIAH
73

16 — THE STORY OF LAZARUS, MARTHA, & MARY
77

17 — THE STORY OF LYDIA
81

18 — THE STORY OF THE MAN BORN BLIND
85

19 — THE STORY OF MIRIAM
91

20 – THE STORY OF NAAMAN
97

21 – THE STORY OF NAOMI
101

22 – THE STORY OF NEHEMIAH
105

23 – THE STORY OF ONESIMUS
111

24 – THE STORY OF PETER & CORNELIUS
117

25 – THE STORY OF THE PREACHER
121

26 – THE STORY OF THE SAMARITAN WOMAN AT THE WELL
127

27 – THE STORY OF STEPHEN
133

28 – THE STORY OF TAMAR
139

29 – THE STORY OF WISDOM
143

30 – THE STORY OF THE WOMAN WHO ANOINTS JESUS
149

About the Author
153

This book is dedicated
to the Core Group of World Harvest Fellowship – Auckland.
You have all inspired me to write and complete this book.

Copyright © 2024 by Danny Ninal
Scripture Quotations marked NIV are taken from the Holy Bible, New International Version, Copyright 1973, 1978, 1984 by International Bible Society. Used by permission of Zondervan. All rights reserved. [Biblica]
All rights reserved. No part of this book may be reproduced in any manner whatsoever without written permission except in the case of brief quotations embodied in critical articles and reviews.
First Printing, 2024

INTRODUCTION

More Than Words is about the Bible, a book that has shaped civilizations, inspired art, and guided countless lives. It's a collection of stories, poetry, history, and prophecy, a tapestry woven with faith, hope, and love threads. But the Bible is more than just words on a page. It's a living, breathing entity, a source of wisdom, comfort, and challenge.

This book, **More Than Words: A Bible Study Guide for New Believers**, invites you to embark on a journey of discovery. We'll delve beyond the surface, exploring the depths of meaning hidden within the pages of Scripture. We'll examine the stories, the characters, the themes, and the profound impact the Bible has had on humanity throughout the ages.

We'll explore the Bible as a timeless guide for navigating the complexities of life. We'll discover how its teachings can answer our most profound questions, offer solace in times of trouble, and ignite a fire of hope within our hearts.

MESSAGE FROM THE AUTHOR

For years, I approached the Bible with a sense of obligation rather than excitement. It felt like a dusty, ancient text, full of stories and teachings that seemed distant and irrelevant to my modern life. I'd read passages, but they rarely resonated with me. I felt like I was missing something profound, something that could truly change my life.

Then, one day, something shifted. I stumbled upon a passage that spoke directly to my struggle. It wasn't just words on a page; it was a lifeline, a source of comfort and hope. At that moment, I realized the Bible wasn't just a book; it was a living, breathing entity, a treasure trove of wisdom and guidance waiting to be discovered.

This book, **The Bible: More Than Words**, reflects that journey. It's an invitation to peel back the layers and explore the hidden depths of Scripture. We'll journey through the pages, not just reading the words but genuinely experiencing them, allowing them to speak to our hearts and minds.

Your word is a lamp for my feet,
A light on my path.
Psalm 119:105 (NIV)

HOW TO USE THIS BOOK

The Bible is good and beautiful. Its vast historical recognition establishes its authority in our collective lives and shows us how its story and storytellers lead us to something bigger than ourselves.

Hearing stories has constantly deepened our understanding of our world. In early Jewish traditions, storytelling is a foundation for flourishing relationships, knowledge, and culture. Deuteronomy 11 (NLT) invites its audience to "commit yourselves wholeheartedly to these words" and "Talk about them when you are at home and when you are on the road, when you are going to bed, and when you are getting up." These early traditions invite us to hear stories as an enduring, generational, and immersive experience.

This invitation from Biblical storytellers should be noticed in our modern society. In today's contexts, it can be easy to reduce this ancient text to brief takeaways or moral to-do lists. But when we choose to see the Bible in this way, we miss out on the fullness of what these stories can be—something wholly sensory and embodied.

We can look to early storytelling traditions as a guide to engaging with the Bible today. The first communities gathered around sacred Bible stories, learning to embody those stories from generation to generation. Art has played a prominent part in this process, transmitting biblical stories and making them meaningful for each new generation. There is wisdom in following the steps of this method—noting how things transpire and allowing them to speak without rush or force.

How to Use This Book

READ Whether heard aloud or in silent reading, hearing the story in its presented form is a bedrock for curiosity, conversation, and relationship.

Reading Chapter

Each chapter's reading section opens with a designated theme, synopsis, and reading list. We invite you to investigate these resources to begin your chapter experience.

Chapter Outline

The chapter then has an outline retelling the story's events. To conclude the readings, we move into the Today section, where we ponder the story and inspect its qualities and themes as they exist in our modern world.

REFLECT Through thoughtful guided prompts, questions, and design, and we invite you to integrate the story into the present and embody a whole experience. Looking to early traditions, we encourage gathering and sharing this experience with others. This section is structured with prompts that will guide you through a process: Pause, Ponder, and Pray.

Pause: Bring awareness to your response to the story. Each chapter has prompts inspired by the story's theme(s) to help guide you through the steps below.

Ponder: Deepen your understanding of the story with questions to reflect on and discuss with your community.

Pray: Close your time with a written prayer uniquely crafted for each chapter. We hope these promptings allow for a more profound experience with the Bible.

Through your study, let there be joy, kinship, and a plentiful connection with goodness and all of creation.

THE FEEDING OF THE FIVE THOUSAND

SATISFYING THE NEEDS

LESSON ONE

SYNOPSIS But many saw them leaving and recognized them, and they hurried on foot from all the towns and arrived there ahead of them. (Mark 6:33 NET)

Read Perhaps it starts as a small trickle of people, picking up steam with each new town they pass. Eventually, like a crowd of marathon runners, they jog in a large, unruly pack of thousands. While some English translations say they "hurried," the original Greek uses a word that could be translated as they ran together or "rushed together." They are running together—people from different towns and families, people with various occupations and life experiences and personalities— united only by their urgent need to be where Jesus is.

What exactly did they need?

First, the crowd needs compassion. When Jesus reaches the other side of the lake, he sees the crowd and feels a *loving pity* for them. In Greek, that's a strong word—literally, Jesus is *moved to the bowels.*

Jesus is moved because he sees that the crowd needs all the sheep need from a shepherd: guidance, wisdom, direction, and safety. They need protection from their predators, who are many—from occupying Roman armies to predatory money lenders and tax collectors to corrupt religious leadership.

The crowd also needs teaching. They hurry around the lake to meet Jesus because they know they must hear what he says. They are hungry to learn how to live. They are starving for peace and wholeness in a violent world, for justice in an unjust world.

And so, Jesus teaches them.

Perhaps the crowd is so transfixed by Jesus' story-telling that, as the day begins to fade to evening, they hardly realize they are hungry for food. Perhaps they have been unable to carry much with them on their long jog around the lake. Most are very materially poor; many may not know where their next meal is coming from.

The disciples ask Jesus to send the crowd away to buy dinner for themselves. But Jesus understands needs are not just spiritual or emotional; they are tangible and material. He asks the disciples to feed the crowd themselves. It is a baffling instruction; they hardly have money for such a feat.

But Jesus isn't concerned about their limited resources. Instead, he wants to help the community find and share what they have. The disciples survey the crowd and report five loaves and two fish.

Jesus thanks God for these communal resources, scant as they may seem. A miracle happens as Jesus breaks the bread and asks his disciples to distribute it to the people. The bread is not running out, and neither is the fish.

Everyone is eating, and everyone has plenty. In the Greeks, people are *filled to the full,* completely satisfied. Their needs are met with surprising, miraculous, communal abundance.

And perhaps this is the one last thing the crowd needs. They need to know that, with God, everyone eats to the full—indeed, everyone—and there are plenty of leftovers. At God's table, everything is shared, and everyone's needs are seen and provided for. At God's banquet, there is no need to compete, push, or shove to be first in line for food. There is only an invitation to sit, rest, and let God provide. The God of Jesus is a God who meets human needs with divine abundance.

TODAY Jesus cares about the entire, holistic needs of people. Today, just as in Jesus' time, many people have needs that go beyond just the spiritual; they have serious material needs too—the need for comfortable and affordable housing, the need for a car, the need for health care, the need for work that pays a live-able wage. Jesus doesn't just callously tell people not to worry about these things; rather, he meets these needs as part of caring for all human beings. He takes tangible steps to make sure no one goes hungry.

As Dante Stewart writes in *Shoutin' in the Fire: An American Epistle:* "When Jesus healed people, he wasn't just concerned about their souls. He was concerned about their bodies. Bodies caught up in oppression and exploitation. Bodies forgotten by the community and the empire. Bodies caught up in the streets."

Jesus cares about *whole* people—and about all people. He cares about the people our society tends to overlook and undervalue.

If God is a God who meets human needs with divine abundance, what does that look like in our communities? Who isn't experiencing this abundance? What are the barriers that keep them from it, and what would it look like for those barriers to be removed? We are united at God's banquet table by our typical neediness. Our needs are part of our humanity; they are nothing to be ashamed of. We are meant to care for others and be cared for by others in healthy, interdependent communities. Across the world, mutual aid networks are doing just that. Ordinary people are coming together creatively and cooperatively to meet each other's needs.

How aware are we of our needs? How willing are we to share our needs with others? What might it look like to bravely and vulnerably name our needs in all forms—and to support others as they do the same?

REFLECT
PAUSE   Sit up straight.
            Take a deep breath.
            Reading the verses today, take a moment to reflect on the story.

PONDER   Invite God to speak to you:

I. What do you think about expressing your needs? What does being open to others and caring for your needs look like?
II. How aware are we of the needs of those around us? Are there people in our society that we may overlook? How can we better understand their needs?
III. How does the feeling of scarcity prohibit us from helping each other? How does Jesus show us that there is abundance today?

PRAYER
Heavenly Father, You are the God of Abundance; help me to believe that You meet the needs of all.
When our bodies grumble, and our legs are tired, may we rest together and be full. In Jesus Name, I pray.
Amen.

ASSIGNMENT: Please read 1 Samuel 25 for Lesson Two

THE STORY OF ABIGAIL

Decisive Action / Subverting Expectations / Non-Violence
1 Samuel 25

LESSON TWO

SYNOPSIS   Abigail is an overlooked hero who takes decisive, subversive action against the violent acts of those around her to save the lives of many.

Read   Abigail's story is set within David's nomadic journey to the throne. David, with a sizable army in Carmel, encounters sheep being sheared. These sheep are the property of Nabal, Abigail's husband. David and his men remain with the flock and the shepherds, protecting Nabal's property with their presence. In return, David asks Nabal for provisions for his army, an expected courtesy for such protection.

Nabal responds with more than a refusal; he insults David.

David's anger flares up in a call to arms. He leaves a third of his army to protect their baggage while the others prepare to confront Nabal and slaughter his entire household.

Abigail is informed of the coming attack and springs into action. Quickly, she has a gift assembled to appease David but does not inform her husband. Wine and bread, dressed sheep and extra grain, raisins, and figs—all are loaded on donkeys and sent off to the coming army with Abigail following closely behind. Perhaps this is a risk she takes, knowing that likely her husband expects her to stay behind and support his decisions. Maybe she is more keenly aware that violence is coming. To Abigail, saving lives was more important than staying in her lane. She bends expectations for the greater good.

So here comes Nabal's wife instead of Nabal himself. When she meets David, Abigail takes responsibility for her husband's audacity and lack of hospitality—although she had nothing to do with it! She acts on behalf of her husband, more than making up for his failure.

Abigail could have sent the gift and hoped for the best. In that moment, Abigail acts despite fear and violence and amid poor decisions made by others. Abigail's pleading for peace shows discernment and foresight.

David applauds her good sense and quick thinking, recognizing that she kept him from violence and releasing her back to her household in peace. The worst is over; tempers fizzle out, and she has saved many lives.

Abigail returns to find her husband still feasting, unaware that death has come knocking on his door. She decides to leave him in ignorance until morning. When she tells him what has happened, Nabal's shock is great, and within ten days, he dies.

On his journey, David hears of Nabal's death and sends for Abigail to be his wife. Abigail consents to the marriage and joins him on his way to the throne.

TODAY In a culture obsessed with celebrity, renown, and prestige, Abigail reminds us it is most often overlooked heroes who make our world a better place. Her story encourages us to act wherever we find ourselves, even when it means coloring outside the lines. She commanded authority without being given it explicitly (by her role in society as a woman). She saw a need and took necessary action to prevent destruction, even when it meant subverting the norms.

Abigail's story also teaches us *how* to take decisive action. So often, when met with an opposing force, our tendency is towards violence. This might not be physical violence outright, however, as Dr. Marshall B. Rosenberg defines it in his book *Non-Violent Communication:*

If 'violent' means acting in ways that result in hurt or harm, then much of how we Communicate— judging others, bullying, having racial bias, blaming, finger-pointing, discriminating, speaking without listening, criticizing others or ourselves, name-calling, reacting when angry, using political rhetoric, being defensive or judging who's 'good/bad' or what's 'right/wrong' with people—could indeed be called 'violent communication.'"

Abigail's swift and decisive actions demonstrate the complete opposite of them. Instead of brashness, she demonstrates listening and intentionality. Instead of hostility, she shows hospitality.

Abigail's story asks us to consider how we respond to the people around us. If the problem is beyond our apparent influence, should we stick to our roles—or do we choose to take decisive action? And how do we take action—do we move in opposition to others, or do we subvert expectations, nonviolently, to serve a greater good?

REFLECT

PAUSE   Sit up straight.
                Take a deep breath.
                Reading the verses today, take a moment to reflect on the story.

PONDER   : Invite God to speak to you:

I. Where do you see yourself in Abigail's story? What parts can you relate to?
II. Are there areas in your life that require swift, decisive action even though it might be subverting norms?
III. What challenges do you have with non-violent communication? In the face of opposition, how can you respond non-violently?

PRAYER

Heavenly Father, You know my heart, and You see my motives, hurts, and dreams.
Help me to see beyond what I can see on the outside, even if that means bending expectations.
Please help me to watch for unexpected moments, for chances to be bold, and to act decisively.
May these moments of boldness and action be within Your will. This I pray in the sweet name of Jesus Christ.
Amen.

ASSIGNMENT: Please read Luke 2:41-52 for Lesson Three

THE STORY OF THE BOY JESUS

Exploration / Growing Up
Luke 2:41-52

LESSON THREE

SYNOPSIS We explore Jesus's childhood story and what it means to love and honor our families while faithfully pursuing God's unique path for us.

Read This story provides us with a rare glimpse into Jesus' childhood. While his birth is documented in great detail, we know little about his upbringing outside of this account. However, it's a vignette rich with insight into a growing Messiah. At twelve years old, we see him discovering his divine calling—much to the confusion of his earthly parents.

Mary and Joseph endured many challenges since the birth of their son, from living as refugees in Egypt to facing the lingering stigma of a pregnancy that preceded marriage. But Jesus' parents remained devout throughout, circumcising him on the eighth day and bringing him to the temple for purification after childbirth. On the latter visit, Simeon and Anna prophesied over the infant Messiah, filling their hearts with wonder and curiosity about his mysterious future.

Until then, though, what would it be like to raise God?

Years later, in today's passage, we find preteen Jesus accompanying his family on their annual trip to Jerusalem for the Passover festival. They make the grueling pilgrimage on foot, traveling in a caravan with other family and community members. We can surmise that Jesus is a social kid because his parents assume he is walking with the other travelers on the first day of their journey home. But they start to panic when he doesn't turn up at nightfall.

Three days of frantic searching pass before they find their son in an unusual circumstance: in the temple court, surrounded by religious scholars. For three days, he has been listening, learning, and asking questions about scripture. The leaders spoke with awe of their son's wisdom and understanding beyond his years.

More relieved than angry, his parents showed him their anxiety. His response is one of innocent confusion: "Why were you searching for me? Didn't you know I had to be in my father's house?"

Jesus can feel a special connection to God even at this young age. He stays behind simply because he wants to be close to his heavenly Father. However, we can only imagine his parents' or his siblings' rejection when he says this. Despite all the prophecies spoken over him, he is still their son, whom they have loved ever since he was a crying baby. In this jarring interaction, he becomes a mystery to them again.

This incident foreshadows the many times in Jesus' ministry when he was misunderstood. Religious leaders would accuse him, crowds would scorn him, and even his disciples would struggle to comprehend him. After a particularly disappointing visit to Nazareth, he remarked, "A prophet is honored everywhere except in his hometown and among his relatives and his own family."

But Jesus never wavered in his calling. Instead, he returned again and again to his father's presence, just as he had as a little boy of twelve years old.

TODAY It's comforting to note that Jesus understands what it's like to be born into a family. This story reminds us that every parent has dreams for their children, and every child longs to make their parents proud. But as we grow, tension naturally begins to build between family expectations and the inescapable reality of who we are.

For those of us who come from a legacy of faith, this process may be complicated by a desire to explore our beliefs in a way that varies from how our parents express theirs. For others, conflicts may arise from where we work, who we choose to be with, or how we spend our time. It can be bewildering when parents become distressed by our efforts to live out the values they instilled in us. What do we do when God leads us in a seemingly contradictory direction?

With so many voices in our ears from this noisy world, it's tempting to fixate on the approval of people we respect while missing God's whispers to us. It feels much safer to go along with what's familiar than to embrace the tension of our journey with Jesus into the wilderness.

Every family must navigate this process of respecting one another while recognizing God has a unique story for each of us. May we honor each person's pilgrimage as we consistently return to where we all belong: our father's house.

REFLECT

PAUSE Sit up straight.

Take a deep breath.

Reading the verses today, take a moment to reflect on the story.

PONDER Invite God to speak to you:

I. What expectations have you experienced from your family growing up? How have you navigated them?

II. Who has been a source of wisdom in your life? What wisdom have they passed down to you?

III. In what areas of your life do you feel invited to explore your own story? How can you make space in your life to do it?

PRAYER

God of all things new, I thank you for watching over me
and sending those to walk before me
so I may find my own story.
Teach me to honor and love the pilgrimage of many.
In your name,
Amen.

ASSIGNMENT: Please read Matthew 15:21-31 for Lesson Four

THE STORY OF THE CANAANITE WOMAN

Persistency
Matthew 15:21-31

LESSON FOUR

SYNOPSIS A Canaanite woman displays agency and persistence as she goes to Jesus in need of healing.

Read The story begins with Jesus withdrawing to the regions of Tyre and Sidon during his busy time in ministry. There, a woman comes to him and shouts with anguish, "Lord, Son of David, have mercy on me! My daughter is demon-possessed and suffering terribly!"

This woman's cry emerges from a deep love and care for her daughter. Her cry is profound; it is a cry laced with faith. This woman's faith is evident from the beginning as she places her body in a dangerous situation, knowing all the harmful implications that could occur in this culture. Being a Gentile woman amongst a group of Jewish men, she is crossing a social boundary by speaking up to a group with more cultural power than she has. Initially, she is met with silence. The silence holds within it her hopes, fears, and anxiousness. Filled with emotion and faith, she persists, so much so that the disciples beg Jesus to send her away.

Jesus finally addresses the woman, and we are caught off guard as he reinforces the line of exclusion, saying, "I was sent only to the lost sheep of Israel."

The woman is blocked in a way. Anyone whose prayers have gone unanswered might feel blocked. And yet, the woman feels the weight of the line and chooses to cross it anyway. She kneels before him and calls him Lord, indicating his lordship over even her.

Indeed, Jesus will answer her wish now! His reply is even harsher: "It is not right to take the children's bread and toss it to the dogs." Jesus appears to reinforce his drawing line and build a wall to render the mother like a dog.

Anyone else would've taken the hint, for the insult must have been felt acutely. Perhaps her breath got shallow, her hands shaking, her forehead full of sweat. But still, the woman refuses to be excluded. "Even the dogs eat the crumbs that fall from their master's table."

While filled with the trauma of the experience, the woman refuses to allow silence, separation, or being equated to an animal to stop her from what she knows she deserves. For this, she is rewarded. Jesus replies, "Woman, you have great faith! Your request is granted." The woman's daughter is healed immediately.

TODAY The Canaanite woman's narrative displays the critical role of agency and persistence in interacting with God. Ultimately, her pushback against a block for the sake of her family resulted in healing.

How many of us feel we can push back against God? Too often, our interactions with God are the opposite— quietly passive and submissive. But this is not the type of partnership God invites us into. The woman's story reminds us we have agency when interacting with God. We can go to God in desperation; we can have friction; we can tussle—this is the stuff of genuine relationships. It may not be effective at first; it may even feel like our dignity is being disrespected despite our sincerity. But the woman's story shows us that our agency in shaping our relationship with God can lead to healing—even in the face of a door that God initially says is closed. The story does not tell us why Jesus rejected the woman. Nevertheless, the story shows us that God does not desire our passivity but leads us into partnership spaces. The most apparent invitation to this kind of relationship between God and God's people is found in the name of Israel. In Hebrew, Israel can be translated as "wrestles (or struggles) with God." The Canaanite woman knew that the God of Israel was a God who invited this kind of engagement and participation. Against cultural expectations, she embodied the spirit of God's people as she engaged Jesus in this messy yet beautiful moment.

This Canaanite woman exemplifies the reality that we don't fully achieve healing on our own, but we are invited to participate and partner with God in our own healing. As we do participate, we experience a type of liberation that acknowledges we have a voice and agency within our mutual relationship with God. We can trust God will meet us in our breath, in our fight, and in our struggle—even in our struggle with God.

REFLECT

PAUSE   Sit up straight.
Take a deep breath.
Reading the verses today, take a moment to reflect on the story.

PONDER   Invite God to speak to you:

I. Where have you felt a lack of agency in your faith life? Where did those barriers come from?
II. When have you come to God with a request, only for it to go unfulfilled? What does it look like to push back with even more faith?

PRAYER

Heavenly Father, our Healer, I come to You again for healing.
May I hold on to your loving arms and never let go.
May my faith cross all barriers,
and Your blessings abound here and now.
I pray for this in the name of Jesus Christ,
my Lord and Savior. Amen.

ASSIGNMENT: Please read Numbers 27:1-11 for Lesson Five

THE STORY OF THE DAUGHTERS OF ZELOPHEHAD

Advocating in Community / Connecting to Our Needs

Numbers 27:1-11

LESSON FIVE

SYNOPSIS This little-known story occurs when the daughters of Zelophehad find themselves with no inheritance or resources but each other. They advocate for their needs and change laws for the better.

Read After a traumatic and awe-inspiring exodus from slavery under the Egyptians, and the Israelites find themselves wandering the Sinai wilderness in search of a promise—a home where they can finally trade roaming for rest.

At this point in their story, the Israelites had experienced uprisings and rebellions, conflicts both internally and with other peoples, and encounters with enemy kings and hostile deities. But the heart of their journey hinges on an important question: What does it mean to be in community with each other?

In this setting, we meet sisters Mahlah, Noah, Hoglah, Micah, and Tirzah. Recently bereaved of their father, Zelophehad, they face an anxious dilemma as unmarried women in a patrilineal system that legally requires male heirs for the transfer of wealth and property. They stand to lose everything because their father has no sons.

However, the sisters recognize that their father's inheritance would best meet their needs for safety, security, and survival resources. The alternative would be to rely on the generosity of their extended family while waiting for their marriages. However, that would also mean that their father's name would end with his death.

So, the sisters take matters into their own hands.

In the presence of Moses, the priests, the leaders, and the congregation of the Israelites openly questioned the Levitical Law set by God and delivered through Moses. They ask, "Why should the name of our father be taken away from his clan because he had no son? Give to us a possession among our father's brothers."

There is no guarantee they would have emerged from that situation unharmed. There are plenty of Old Testament examples of people God strikes down for disrespect or disobedience. Their request to retain their father's inheritance directly challenges the parameters God had set for the community.

Moses presents their case before God, and God affirms that the sisters are right to bring their petition and agree to meet their needs. God does not simply make a notable exception but further instructs Moses to change the law to meet the community's evolving needs. From that point on, "if a man dies and has no son, then give his inheritance on to his daughters," God commands.

These sisters took account of their needs and found the determination to advocate for themselves in a system that was not created to consider them. And not only did they get their needs met and change the system for themselves, but it was also changed for those that came after them.

TODAY It may be a surprise that a book like Numbers—tucked away between genealogies, legal codes, and ritual requirements for worship—would invite us to consider what it means to advocate for our needs in a communal space.

As modern readers, we may not quite see how brave these sisters' actions were at face value. Advocating for their needs as women without the support of a man was a courageous act in a patriarchal community. While our surroundings may be different than Mahlah, Noah, Hoglah, Micah and Tirzah, many of us confront similar obstacles in a world that often demands we find the courage to speak or to act on behalf of ourselves.

We may feel a deep conviction inside us but find that conviction unwelcome in specific spaces. Depending on who we are and where we are, certain powers and principalities may prefer us to be silent and disconnected from our voices and needs.

Yet our world craves examples of those who choose to nurture and connect to their own needs. It's too easy to stay disconnected from our inner voice and allow certain norms to dictate our futures. But those who remain attentive to their own needs, like the sisters in this story, have the opportunity to forge their path forward—a path that others can follow.

Working out our needs in the community does not mean that our advocacy results in immediate results. It is hard work. It does not always come in the form we expect. It takes time, effort, and grit to see it through. At times, we may feel constrained by forces bent on keeping us insecure and overwhelmed. Yet we are called by God's voice to know ourselves and others in the community as we ask for what we need.

This little-known story from Numbers reminds us that when we find ourselves in unfavorable community spaces, choosing to advocate for ourselves anyway might yield unexpected results. Learning to advocate for our needs can improve our circumstances and provide for the needs of those who come after us. Like the sisters, perhaps we have the most significant impact when we advocate for what we need in the community.

REFLECT

PAUSE   Sit up straight.
Take a deep breath.
Reading the verses today, take a moment to reflect on the story.

PONDER   Invite God to speak to you:

I. Have there been times when you have gone from neglecting your needs to connecting to them? What does connecting to your needs and advocating for them look like?
II. Do you have a community where you share resources and needs and take action together? Where do you find these communities?
III. How do today's systems and constructs not meet our needs (physical, spiritual, emotional), and how do we meet them for ourselves and our communities?

PRAYER

Heavenly Father, You see everything.
Would You please see us when our needs are not met?
You hear everything. Would you listen to us
when we advocate for ourselves and each other?
Empower us to make new things happen
so your people can live fully and freely.
Amen.

ASSIGNMENT: Please read Judges Chapters 4 & 5 for Lesson Six

THE STORY OF DEBORAH

Bravery
Judges 4:4-24

LESSON SIX

SYNOPSIS As a brave prophet, Deborah guides the people of Israel from the front lines of a battle to end their suffering.

Read The story picks up when the people of Israel forego their commitment to live in step with God. Choosing this straying path—evil over love, selfishness instead of mercy—leads them to suffer under the oppressive rule of King Jabin and his commander Sisera.

At this time comes the prophet and leader, Deborah. Deborah's role in her community was to speak wisdom into situations of injustice. Day after day, she'd sit under a large palm tree and tend to men and women seeking wisdom and sound judgment.

One day, Deborah summons the military commander Barak, relaying God's message to prepare for battle and to gather the troops. It was time for the people to break free and fight Sisera's army!

The enormity of the situation overwhelms Barak; while he trusts Deborah, he wants her to accompany him to rally the troops. "If you go with me, I will go, but if you don't, I won't." Deborah bravely says she will but also calls out Barak's wavering spirit and responds with a prophetic promise—it won't be him, but "the hands of a woman" who will defeat Sisera.

Barak and Deborah begin to gather a large army to wage battle for the flourishing of their people. Word gets back to Sisera that they are preparing for war, so Sisera gathers nine hundred iron chariots. Deborah strategically tells Barak to get ready, knowing that, by the grace of God, this oppressive army will lead them right where Barak needs them. She is full of assured confidence in God, telling Barak: "Go! This is the day the Lord has given Sisera into your hands. Has not the Lord gone ahead of you?"

And that's precisely what happens. The armies of Israel are given prime opportunity to strike. Victory is theirs. No soldier from Sisera's army is spared, and Sisera himself flees, running for his life and taking shelter within the tent of one of his nation's allies—Heber and his wife, Jael.

Jael welcomes him and agrees not to alert anyone. That night, Sisera falls asleep, and seeing an opportunity, Jael kills him by driving a tent peg through his temple. Thus, she fulfills Deborah's prophecy to Barak—a woman's hand will kill Sisera.

Deborah and Barak celebrate! A joyous song is sung to usher in forty years of peace in the land and is etched into history as one of the oldest written excerpts of Scripture.

TODAY Like Deborah, we are invited to be people of bravery even amidst impossible odds. She had every reason to doubt whether it was the 900 iron chariots lined before her, dealing with intense quarrels among her people, or needing to garner command over numerous men in power. But instead of fear, Deborah exemplifies the complete opposite. She exudes confidence and authority as she boldly listens to God, wielding her courage to free her people.

We are reminded of many civil rights movement leaders rooted in these qualities, like Fannie Lou Hamer. As a devoted faith leader and Black woman in the 1960s South, Fannie Lou Hamer was part of a marginalized community living under oppressive and racist systems and structures. Though she was threatened, arrested, and subject to violence, it never deterred her from her life's work. She was brave, continually putting her body on the line with civil acts of disobedience to expose inequities and inequalities.

When dire times call for bravery, how do we respond? God does not leave us, even when we are most afraid. We can trust that the Spirit will empower us in truth and righteousness when we need to be brave. Barak wavered to rally the troops—but Deborah was there, ready, trusting God—and so was Jael. Contrast Barak's trepidation with Deborah's confidence. As she commands Barak, she says: "Has not the Lord gone ahead of you?" Such a rhetorical question reveals her confidence in God, and she gets to experience that confidence fully realized in victory.

When we choose fear, we miss out on opportunities in life; we shrink and diminish below what God intends for us. But when we select bravery, we get to live in step with God and experience life's fullness. What is stirring your soul, spurring you on to act bravely? Be brave; perhaps it will lead to a wondrous chorus.

REFLECT

PAUSE   Sit up straight.
Take a deep breath.
Reading the verses today, take a moment to reflect on the story.

PONDER   Invite God to speak to you:

I. Where are you invited to be brave? How can you rise to God's call for bravery?
II. What stirs your soul and makes you sing? How can it help you live bravely?
III. How can we wield our courage from God to bring freedom to ourselves and others?

PRAYER

You alone, God, are my strength.
With each step with You, my soul is stirred, and my heart sings.
Grant me bravery when I am faced with hardships.
And may I join in the divine melody of life with You. Amen.

ASSIGNMENT: Please read Luke Chapter 1 for Lesson Seven

THE STORY OF ELIZABETH

Waiting With Hope
Luke 1

LESSON SEVEN

SYNOPSIS While experiencing significant pressures and challenges amidst her maternal journey, Elizabeth waits with hope and expectation for the fulfillment of her desire to have a child.

Read Luke begins the story by elevating the character of Elizabeth and her husband, Zachariah. Both are described as righteous before God, "careful to obey all the commandments and regulations."1 Yet, they deal with the uncomfortable reality of barrenness, which in Jewish culture was commonly viewed as an indicator of personal sin and punishment from God (i.e., Lev 20:20). In Elizabeth's old age, with no physical signs of conceiving, she carried that stigma every day.

But despite co-existing in the tension of being both blameless and childless, she lived a faith-filled life, quietly holding the desire of one day bearing a child close to her heart for many years.

Then, one day, unexpectedly, her husband comes home mute after encountering the angel Gabriel, who prophesies they will have a son.2 A son who will be a great prophet, filled with the Holy Spirit, and who will set the stage for the coming Messiah. Soon after, Elizabeth conceives this foretold baby and spends five months in seclusion.

Why choose seclusion upon hearing this blessed news? Was she waiting for her pregnancy to be visible to the rest of the world as a physical sign? Was she spending her time undistracted in prayer and praise with God? Though uncertain, Elizabeth continued to wait like the many years before she conceived.

In the sixth month of Elizabeth's pregnancy, her cousin Mary encounters the angel Gabriel, who tells her she will miraculously conceive Jesus. When Mary visits Elizabeth, her baby leaps into the womb the moment Mary's voice meets Elizabeth's ears. The Holy Spirit fills Elizabeth with joy, and she pronounces a blessing. With Elizabeth's testimony present and fully showing in her rounded belly, the Holy Spirit allows her to immediately recognize the similar favor God has bestowed upon Mary—to carry the One all of Israel has been waiting

for. Elizabeth is hopeful that the end of waiting to see her Messiah is on the horizon.

Elizabeth's waiting is met with a fulfilled promise—a child they name John (whom we come to know as John the Baptist). Her community, who previously shunned and shamed her, gathered around to rejoice with her in this miraculous event.

TODAY Waiting is not easy. Waiting with hope is even more complicated when faced with seemingly impossible circumstances. But it is a virtue that keeps our spirits alive and ready to receive when our desires are finally fulfilled.

Elizabeth's display of waiting with hope reminds us of the stories of many people who find themselves wrongfully shamed, blamed, or physically shunned. In 1992, Ray Krone was sentenced to prison for a murder he did not commit. He spent a total of 10 years moving around different Arizona prisons and 32 months on death row. In 2002, when a DNA test was finally conducted, Krone was found innocent. On the day of his release, Krone's mother conversed with a reporter, remarking that their family would set a place at the table for Ray, waiting patiently for him to come home every Thanksgiving and Christmas. While Krone's physical circumstances appeared highly unfavorable, his mother held onto the hope that her son would be found innocent and eventually released, and so he was.

In her waiting, Elizabeth served God and even secluded herself until her pregnancy began, just as Ray's mother set a place at the table for him every year. Both individuals did not know how their stories would end, but that didn't prevent them from accepting the possibility of their desires coming to fruition.

We all have things we are waiting for. Elizabeth's story is an invitation to stay—not with pessimism, cynicism, or negativity—but full of hope, knowing the God of fulfillment is with us.

REFLECT

PAUSE   Sit up straight.
Take a deep breath.
Reading the verses today, take a moment to reflect on the story.

PONDER   Invite God to speak to you:

I. What are you waiting for most urgently? What role does hope have in your waiting?
II. Where is God in your waiting? How do you spend your time with God when you are waiting?
III. When have you kept your time waiting between you and God? When have you invited the community into your waiting time?

PRAYER
Heavenly Father, You are beyond time.
Help me wait faithfully and remain hopeful,
for you can do everything, even when they feel insurmountable.
May I seek you when I wait for you, seek community in the waiting,
and celebrate with others. Amen.

ASSIGNMENT: Please read Esther Chapters 4-7 for Lesson Eight.

THE STORY OF ESTHER

Courage / God's Providence
Esther 4-7

LESSON EIGHT

SYNOPSIS The story of Esther is about a woman whose life was caught up in circumstances and traumas bigger than herself, who acted with courage to save her people and, amidst it all, shined a light on a God working behind the scenes.

Read Esther's story was historically conceived to recount the significance of the Jewish festival of Purim. Purim can be translated to "lots," a form of decision-making that appears to be made by chance. This quality shapes much of Esther's story, celebrating the mysterious intermingling of chance and divine providence.

The story begins with Esther being plucked out from under the care of her uncle, Mordecai, and placed in the fortress of Susa, getting prepared to be presented to King Xerxes as a potential wife. The "preparation" is traumatic—she has no choice and no authority in the circumstance, and Mordecai, aware that her Jewish nationality could put her in danger in the king's courts, advises her to keep her heritage a secret. So, there she is, without her family, disconnected from her people, and without any choice—being presented (amongst many other women) to King Xerxes.

To everyone's surprise, King Xerxes favors Esther and makes her the queen. What are the odds?

Here in the story, we're introduced to another character, Haman, who is promoted to the most powerful official in the empire.2 After a tense encounter and feeling disrespected by Mordecai, Haman hatches a plot to destroy the Jewish people. He brings his plan to the king, alleging the Jewish people refuse to follow the king's laws. King Xerxes agrees with Haman and signs a decree, declaring a day in the future as the day all of the Jewish people in the Persian Empire should be killed.

Where is Esther in all of this?

Well, she's unaware the decree was signed. When she hears her uncle Mordecai is distressed, she tries to find out why. She finds out that her people, who are courageously resisting their captivity, are now set to be killed by the king. In step with the spirit of her community, she conceives of a plan to resist this order, but it would require her to put herself in danger in the court willingly—no one, including the queen, is allowed to enter the king's court uninvited. Seeing the dangerous circumstances in front of her, Esther asks Mordecai to gather their people to fast and pray for her as she prepares to present herself before the king.

While her people are fasting, Esther devises a plan to persuade the king to save her people, incriminating Haman in the process. During the second feast she requests, while they are all drinking wine, Esther reveals that her people are set to be killed and that Haman instigated it all.

In that moment, Esther risks her life by identifying herself as a member of the people set to be killed. She risks vulnerability in the hope that it will change the king's mind. And it does. The story ends triumphantly, with her uncle Mordecai being put into a position of power and her people gaining the right to fight for themselves.

Esther began this story in a place of trauma. She had no choice or authority and was disconnected from her people. The odds were stacked against her and her community. But this story ends with a resilient tone. Though her people still faced many challenges of captivity, her commitment to her community saved their lives, keeping them from experiencing a collective trauma—death.

Where is God in all of this?

God goes unmentioned in the story in all its twists and turns. This might seem strange at first—for something within the Biblical canon—but here lies its brilliance. Through all its twists, turns, and chance-filled moments lies a picture of God working behind the scenes, setting up the salvation of the Jewish people.

TODAY Looking to Esther as a guide, we see courage as something that simultaneously takes vulnerability, community, and time. This story reminds us of all of the communities faced with injustice in recent history who turned to their own for support. Over many years, women with Esther's qualities courageously fought to gain the right to vote in the United States in the '20s. In the civil rights movement in the '50s and '60s, many Black Americans organized their communities, fighting for a more inclusive society. These courageous movements did not happen overnight— it took significant commitment and support from one another.

Esther went through a multi-day process to build the courage to speak up. She asked for her community's help through fasting and prayer and what's at stake?

Esther's story is compelling because of the "divine chance" embedded in the narrative. She just happened to become a queen who heard about a plot to kill her people and had enough favor with the king to do something about it. Amid seemingly random occurrences, God was at work behind the scenes, setting up liberation.

As we ponder on our lives today, there is a possibility that beneath the surface, God is setting us up for something great. The question is: do we have eyes to see it?

REFLECT
PAUSE Sit up straight.
Take a deep breath.
Reading the verses today, take a moment to reflect on the story.

PONDER Invite God to speak to you:

I. Where do you hope God works behind the scenes in your life?
II. Are there any circumstances you're scared of and need courage?
III. How can you connect to the community around you in difficult circumstances?
IV. Where do you have a platform to speak up for others in your life?

PRAYER
God who works behind the scenes,
grant me the courage of Esther.
Give me eyes to see where I can join in with God's love for all people.
Amen.

ASSIGNMENT: Please read Genesis 16 for Lesson Nine.

THE STORY OF HAGAR

Seeing Others / Value
Genesis 16

LESSON NINE

SYNOPSIS A pregnant Hagar flees amidst a threat to her and her child's existence; while in the wilderness, an angel sees her and shares God's vision for her future.

Read Hagar's story begins wrapped up between Abram and Sarai. God has promised to make Abram and Sarai a great nation with many descendants. But a decade has passed, and they still bear no children. In an act of desperation and dismissal of God's promise, Sarai decides to take matters into her own hands. She exercises authority over her maidservant, Hagar, to serve as a surrogate mother—giving her to her husband, Abram, in hopes of having descendants through Hagar.

Soon, Hagar becomes pregnant, and Sarai—out of jealousy and anger—despises and mistreats her. Hagar finds herself in a subservient position, alone as an enslaved woman. But in an act of her agency, Hagar flees into the wilderness.

There, the angel of the Lord earnestly seeks Hagar. The angel asks questions with great compassion and care as the angel lets Hagar tell her story.

"Where have you come from, and where are you going?"

The questions spur Hagar and invite her to search for identity, belonging, and acknowledgment of her lived reality. Of course, the angel already knows the answer to them! Yet the angel gives Hagar a voice and an opportunity to feel seen.

"I am running away…"

What is an enslaved, pregnant woman to do in the desert with no provisions, no possessions, and no covering in a patriarchal, enslaving society? She finds herself in the desert of her despair. But the angel comforts, values, and gives her vision for her future.

The angel says she will have descendants that are too many to count. And she will have a son named Ishmael— whose name means "God hears." The angel sees Hagar's difficult situation but declares a new story for her. In an act of gratitude and praise, Hagar responds to her son's naming with God's naming. She raises her voice and is the first recorded person—and woman—to name God El Roi, which means, "You are the God who sees me." She becomes a mother of the faith for all those who have had to leave home because home was unsafe. All who had to leave their country because their country was not safe. She sees God, and God sees her.

TODAY We find a lot of "firsts" in the story of Hagar. We have the first recorded revelation of an angel of the Lord. We see the first time the angel performs an "ultrasound" in Scripture. We see the first time an angel names a child while still in the mother's womb.

Amidst her strenuous circumstances, God makes Hagar, whose name means "the foreigner," the story's center—providing for Hagar and giving her a new future. While Sarai only saw Hagar as an instrument to make herself great, God truly sees Hagar as a wholly loved and cherished human being. This demonstrates what it means to see others—to find value in them as children of God.

The story of Hagar urges us to ask questions about who we choose to value and bring to the center of our narratives. Who is the last? The lost? The least? The lonely? The misunderstood? The mistreated? Do we see these people?

We live in a fractured moment in history—there are more refugees than at any time in history; as the wealth gap increases, there are more and more people being left behind. Amidst these pains, we can look to Hagar as a mother of the faith and find comfort that God values and centers those most often forgotten. God's eyes never stop seeking and searching for those in need—and we, too, are invited to know this, and then do the same. How do we choose to value others? How do we come alongside our strangers and ask questions of compassion: where have you come from, and where are you going?

Pray for the Holy Spirit to help you see with the Seeing One.

REFLECT

PAUSE   Sit up straight.
Take a deep breath.
Reading the verses today, take a moment to reflect on the story.

PONDER   Invite God to speak to you:

I. When was there a moment in time where you felt unseen, then or now?
II. How can the community of God's people embody the name of "The God who sees?
III. Who are the unseen around you? How can you make them the center of your story?

PRAYER

To the God who sees me and sees every tear I have ever shed;
thank you for never taking your eyes off of me.
Give us eyes to see the person next to us who feels unseen.
Help us find their value. Help us not to give into despair
or be paralyzed by injustice.
Grant us peace even as we work for peace. Amen.

ASSIGNMENT: Please read 1 Samuel 1:1-20 for Lesson Ten.

THE STORY OF HANNAH

Sorrow / Cultivating Hope
1 Samuel 1:1-20

LESSON TEN

SYNOPSIS A childless woman, Hannah, faces an uncertain future; with hope, she offers her sorrow to God year after year and experiences transformation along the way.

Read Hannah is introduced as "a woman who is deeply troubled." She was one of Elkanah's two wives, the other of whom was named Penninah. Hannah endured the humiliation of seeing her husband's father have multiple children with his other wife while she remained childless. Perhaps Hannah had a deep longing to feel those first flutters that flower into tiny kicks inside her belly; possibly she longed to give birth to a child that had her eyes and Elkanah's hands. But her pain deepened each time Penninah attained what it seemed she could not.

Hannah's trouble may have also been driven by the social and economic consequences of being childless. In this hierarchical and patriarchal society, Hannah's gender alone made her vulnerable and placed her on the margins of society. Being unable to bear children would have been seen as yet another mark against Hannah, pushing her further to the edge of the community. Furthermore, upon the death of their husbands, women relied on their children—particularly their sons—for their protection and economic provision of their everyday needs. Who would care for Hannah in her old age if she had no children? Hannah's present standing within her community and future hinged on her ability to bear children. Hannah was distraught indeed.

Hannah's husband, Elkanah, made some attempts to console his wife. When the household traveled to Shiloh to sacrifice to God, Elkanah gave Hannah "a double portion," presumably more than he gave to Peninnah and her children, to give back to the Lord. Elkanah may have wanted to show his love for Hannah, though she remained without children, but Hannah could not be consoled—all she could do was weep. Even food had lost its appeal. Seeing Hannah's distress, Peninnah did not respond with kindness or empathy. She chastised and humiliated Hannah, which undoubtedly only deepened Hannah's anguish. This was Hannah's life, locked in a cycle of despair.

But amid her weeping, Hannah practiced going to the Lord's house year after year. She was relentless. What else could Hannah do? Facing an uncertain future, she sought the only one who could hold every tear she had ever cried but also the only one who could provide the child for whom she prayed.

During one particular trip to the temple, it seems the grief that took up residence in Hannah's heart is especially exposed, and her sense of desperation is particularly perceptible. She rushes past Eli, the priest sitting outside, tears flowing from her eyes. In this moment, her surroundings and her appearance are unimportant. Out of the depths of her distress, "she prayed to the Lord weeping bitterly."

Hannah offers up both her pain and her petition to God. She asks that God see her misery and give her the son for whom she had prayed for years. She offers the child not conceived back to God—the only giver of life. Her prayers are so fervent that Eli believes her to be drunk. Hannah quickly corrects him. It is not a wine that has been poured out, but her soul. Hannah's appetite returns after baring her sorrow before God, and a smile finally graces her lips. She rejoins her husband, and they eat and drink together. Hannah's circumstances are the same: she has no child, only her tears before God. But God is beginning to transform her.

We need to find out precisely how many years Hannah waits. How many times did she return to the temple, her eyes filled with tears but her womb empty? What the text does make clear is that God answered Hannah's prayers. "Over time," the Lord remembered Hannah, and she gave birth to a son named Samuel. Hannah's weeping turned to joy as she prayed, "There is no Holy One like the Lord, there is no one besides you; there is no Rock like our God.

TODAY Hannah was a woman who knew sorrow. We may not all be able to relate to the particularities of Hannah's story as an Ancient Near Eastern woman relegated to the margins of society by her gender and childlessness. However, each of us knows of pain and suffering. As individuals and communities, we will experience grief differently in kind, frequency, and degree. We lose loved ones to death or broken relationships. We wrestle with addiction, disease, depression, and anxiety. We suffer under the weight of injustice because of where we are born, the color of our skin, whom we love, or because we are poor. Sorrow will find us all.

What, then, will we do when it comes?

Sometimes, weeping turns to singing, as it did for Hannah. When that happens, it is cause for celebration and great joy. But sometimes prayers go unanswered; like Hannah, we have only uncertainty and pain. Sorrow can be a greedy companion, demanding all our energy, diminishing our capacity to hope, and drying up our faith. It can seem complicated, if not impossible, for hope to spring up amid sorrow.

But Hannah's story teaches us to cultivate hope even as the tears flow and our prayers go unanswered. Despite her situation, she practiced prayer and a posture of radical honesty before God, not just on one occasion but year after year. We, too, are free to bring every ounce of our pain before God, who can hold every kind of sorrow—that of our own lives and the kind we hold in solidarity with our neighbors. We can believe we are not shouting into the ether when we pray. Instead, we speak to the Universe's Creator and the Giver of Life. God sees our anguish and knows it for himself. We don't pray only for the removal of pain. Instead, the regular and relentless practice of prayer gives voice to our deepest distresses— and through it transforms us into people who can find joy despite pain.

REFLECT
PAUSE Sit up straight.
Take a deep breath.
Reading the verses today, take a moment to reflect on the story.
PONDER Invite God to speak to you

I. Have any circumstances in your life brought you sorrow recently?
II. What would it look like for us as individuals and as a community to embody Hannah's practice of prayer and posture of radical honesty before God? What steps can you take toward that this week?
III. Where do you see opportunities to listen and hold the anguish of others in your community?

PRAYER
God of sorrow, give me the relentless faith of Hannah.
Teach me to trust You with every ounce of my grief
and to hold the sorrow of others.
We long to know joy again as we wait for our prayers to be answered.
Amen.

ASSIGNMENT: Please read Genesis 33 for Lesson Eleven.

THE STORY OF JACOB & ESAU

Accepting Grace
Genesis 33

LESSON ELEVEN

SYNOPSIS After stealing his brother Esau's inheritance, Jacob lives life under threat and learns what it means to accept grace from his adversaries.

Read Born to Rebekah and Isaac, Jacob was the younger twin of his brother Esau. The story of his birth gives the reader some immediate clues to the complex status he will hold in life; God tells Rebekah that the two born of her "will be separated" and that "one people will be stronger than the other, and the older will serve the younger." As the twins are delivered, Jacob comes out clutching the heel of his brother Esau. This birth account sets the stage for his tale of mistakes, trauma, wounds, and transformation.

Their saga begins as Jacob, jealous of his brother's birthright as the firstborn, sets out to steal a blessing of inheritance meant for Esau. In a moment that sounds as far-fetched as it does dramatic, Jacob tricks his aging, semi-blind father by impersonating Esau during the blessing ritual. This act of deception confers the blessing upon Jacob, by which Esau is understandably enraged.

With his life under threat by Esau, Jacob flees. The estranged brothers spend many years apart, building their families and amassing their wealth. Jacob continues his pattern of duplicity, in desperate bid after bid to prove his worthiness to himself and others. In doing so, he embroils himself in numerous deadly conflicts while never entirely escaping the cast of Esau's shadow.

The height of their conflict reaches its peak as Jacob learns that Esau is coming with four hundred men to exact revenge on him and his family. Jacob splits up his wives, children, and servants, commands them to stay behind, and walks out to meet Esau's company. He is prepared to die at the hands of his brother.

But Jacob does not get what he expects. Instead of being met with violence and rage, the story says that "Esau ran to meet Jacob and embraced him; he threw his arms around his neck and kissed him. And they wept." What Jacob anticipated as the end of the road, the death of the blessing, the loss of the promise, was not the final word.

Still, perhaps because of his traumas, Jacob does not fully recognize the grace Esau offers him. He still feels the pull of old fears and insecurities. Esau offers to travel alongside him, but Jacob responds: "So let my lord go on ahead of his servant while I move along slowly at the pace of the flocks and herds before me and according to the pace of the children." Jacob is communicating something about his fear, albeit indirectly. He is anticipating, even after Esau's embrace, that his brother will come up from behind to kill him as if the grace is too good to be true or too farfetched to be trusted.

Jacob is wrong. Instead of rejection, it is a reunion. Instead of abandonment, it is affection. The relationship is both reassured and reconciled. He has to learn how to accept grace from an unexpected source.

TODAY God seems to pay particular attention to controversial people, and the character of Jacob is no exception. His story is marked by self-doubt, insecurity, and fraud. His choices throughout his life are not parables of virtue or exemplary in any way. Yet his role in forming the Jewish people could not be overstated. Not long before the beginning of our passage, he was renamed Israel by an angel, and he went on to be the father of the twelve tribes of Israel. These kinds of complex people are mixed up in God's story.

As we recall our moments of crisis, we may discover a part of Jacob in all of us. Many of us know exactly what it is like to come into this world clutching the ankle of someone else's promise and blessing. Others of us have been victimized because of who we are or what we look like. Still, some of us face the consequences of our mistakes, confronted with how we have hurt others.

The grace of this story for our lives today is that just as Esau looks on Jacob with unexpected tenderness, the heart of God also sees something different about ourselves than we do. When we are haunted by the ghosts of our past and convinced that our traumas are eternal, God sees us with an eye for beauty. It is this grace that gives Jacob cause to exclaim to Esau, "For to see your face is like seeing the face of God [. . .] for God has been gracious to me." Jacob learns to accept grace.

The opportunity in this story is to remember that grace is available to us, and we must also learn to accept it in all its forms.

REFLECT

PAUSE Sit up straight.
Take a deep breath.
Reading the verses today, take a moment to reflect on the story.

PONDER Invite God to speak to you

I. Where does your own story feel complicated? Are there ways in which you feel burdened by your past?
II. Do you believe love is abundant? What prevents you from accepting grace for yourself? From others? From God?

PRAYER

Gracious God, I open myself to you.
Amidst all the wrongdoings, may I seek to know your love is abundant.
Today and tomorrow, may I see this world with your eyes.
Amen.

ASSIGNMENT: Please read Exodus 18:13-27 for Lesson Twelve.

THE STORY OF JETHRO & MOSES

Wisdom Amidst Successes
Exodus 18:13-27

LESSON TWELVE

SYNOPSIS   Jethro gives his son-in-law, Moses, practical wisdom on governing their newly liberated nation amidst the burdensome challenges that come with great success.

Read   We pick up our story at the height of Moses' success. He had just led the nation of Israel out of slavery in Egypt, parted the Red Sea, watched God feed thousands with manna and produce water from a rock, and won his first battle against the Amalekites. God has been faithful!

Chapter 18 reintroduces an unexpected character, Moses's father-in-law, Jethro. When Jethro visits, he cannot help but praise the Lord for his faithfulness and blessings. When Jethro hears Moses' story and all that God has done, he recognizes the greatness of the God of Israel and offers sacrifices to the Lord. They celebrate what God has done with a sprawling feast that all the elders of Israel attend.

The next day, however, Jethro is alarmed by Moses' leadership style. From dawn till dusk, Moses sits as a judge for the people. He hears all the disputes and conflicts pooled from the thousands of people he led out of Egypt. Jethro asks why Moses is doing all this.

Moses replied that the people were coming to him to hear the will of God.

Despite Moses' successes—all of which are genuinely praiseworthy—Jethro has a deep concern for his son-in-law. "What you are doing is not good," Jethro says, "You and these people who come to you will only wear yourselves out. The work is too heavy for you; you cannot handle it alone."

Pause for a moment and realize to whom Jethro is speaking. This is Moses, the prophet of God, Egypt's plague-bringer, who parted the Red Sea. Even more, Jethro understands Moses's more profound character development. Jethro knew that Moses fled after an Israelite slave mocked him, saying, "Who made you ruler and judge over us?" He knew Moses felt inadequate and inarticulate. He also heard how even the Israelite leaders criticized Moses by saying, "May the Lord look on you and judge you!" Moses' growth and struggle finally led to him being the respected judge of Israel, speaking the word of the Lord.

But even amidst Moses's life's success, Jethro sees his son-in-law's limits. It would've been so easy to be a yes-man to the budding leader of a nation. Jethro, however, vigilantly seeks Moses' holistic flourishing. To keep Moses from burning out, Jethro shares three pieces of wisdom.

First, he affirms Moses as the people's representative before God. Second, he encourages Moses to teach the people to discern God's will for themselves. And third, he instructs Moses to delegate his position as a judge to other capable, God-fearing individuals.

Moses implements this advice, and his workload is made manageable. Because of this simple yet tricky conversation, Jethro forever changes the format of Israel's governance. Here, we experience a picture of a community flourishing together, sharing wisdom, and living humbly before God and each other.

TODAY We are blessed to live in a time when we have countless ways to make a better world. The internet allows us to build relationships with people anywhere on the globe. Social media allows us to influence hundreds of people with a button. We have jobs that provide helpful services to others.

These structures and systems allow us to pursue good things. Similar to Moses, however, we may mistakenly justify working past our limits if it is for a "good thing." Perhaps we even lean on our past successes, capabilities, and triumphs as rationalizations for toiling further. Jethro's invitation for Moses—and all of us—is to let go of the continual need to strive for more, to lean on others, and to be at peace with God.

Additionally, our culture teaches us that being a good supporter means telling people they can do more. We often goad people on to striving for more success without thinking of our friends' well-being or caring for their souls. Everyone wants to encourage, but being a voice of discerning wisdom is more complicated. Cinema and stories have told us that the sidekick always encourages their hero to be the best, the strongest, or the most powerful.

This is different from Jethro's model of wisdom. Jethro knows that Moses needs others to help him as he pursues the blessings of his nation. He has Moses divest the authority and the success given to him by other capable people. Jethro cares more deeply for Moses' soul than his success or power. We, too, are invited to look after others like Jethro. Do we see others beyond their external achievements? Do we speak up when we see them struggling internally? In doing so, we show the very care of God.

REFLECT
PAUSE   Sit up straight.
Take a deep breath.
Reading the verses today, take a moment to reflect on the story.
PONDER   Invite God to speak to you

I. What good things has God done in your life? Celebrate those.
II. In your pursuit of more success or blessings, are there ways you are struggling, overworking, or burning out?
III. Are there people you trust to speak wisdom into your life? Please send a message to thank them for caring for you.
IV. Do people trust you to speak wisdom into their lives? Could you let me know how you've done so?

PRAYER
God of freedom, teach me to be free from pursuing *more*.
I pray for humility, rest, and the wisdom
to let go of something I am not meant to carry.
I pray for courage and the words to speak life
into the lives of others.
Teach me to rest in your love, God,
who has first loved me. Amen.

ASSIGNMENT: Please read Luke 3:1-20 for Lesson Thirteen.

THE STORY OF JOHN THE BAPTIST

Repentance
Luke 3:1-20

LESSON THIRTEEN

SYNOPSIS The prophet, John the Baptist, prepares for the coming Messiah and calls the crowd of people to repentance.

Read Somewhere along the Jordan River, the word of God comes to a man in the wilderness—a man we know as John the Baptist. This defining moment begins a call to ministry and makes way for God's coming kingdom.

Reverberating on the hills of the Judean wilderness, John, recalling the words of the prophet Isaiah, speaks of preparing and cultivating the soil of the people's hearts. The way is to be smooth and ready— every valley filled in, every high place made low, and every obstacle removed. His declarations are a visual metaphor for a message of equity, which calls for justice for the oppressed, commands care for the poor, and rebukes people who wrongly use their power. His invitation echoes far beyond the banks of the Jordan River, calling all to repent and be baptized.

Many hear his call and come to be baptized. However, upon seeing the crowd, John rebukes them harshly, calling them a "brood of vipers". He sees that these people are simply trying to "flee from the coming wrath," and he suggests their injustices and predatory behaviors have no place in God's coming kingdom. Despite his severe rebuke, he offers them a way forward: to bear good fruit in keeping with repentance. It is a plea to change—or the axe lies ready to cut down every tree bearing rotten fruit.

When John utters these harsh words, the people collectively reflect, "What should we do?" John tells them that the path to repentance is to live justly: to share their clothing and food with those who have none and not to extort or take advantage of others. Speaking to a diverse crowd that includes the rich and the poor, as well as tax collectors and soldiers—John wants them to change.

With these directions, John boldly declares a baptism of repentance—not merely submerging into the water but immersion into the love, justice, and tangible care for others. Responding to the crowd's murmuring of a coming Messiah, John speaks of another baptism by the Holy Spirit. John continues to preach his baptism of repentance and the good news of a future Messiah until a threatened King Herod arrests him.

TODAY At its core, the story of John the Baptist is an invitation to repent—to change one's mind. Like John, we are invited to call others to repent. Surprisingly to many, John's call to repentance is not about accepting a set of abstract theological principles. Instead, it's about turning away from selfishness and exploitation—and locating the real needs of the most vulnerable among us. To share clothes and food, and not to take advantage of or threaten others.

How often do we call out the perpetrator when we see injustice and suffering worldwide? Do we remain silent and complacent? When we stay silent, it may be out of a desire for peace. However, more often than not, our silence helps the perpetrator and leaves victims feeling more alone and forgotten. Instead, John demonstrates a radical boldness to call people to the ethics that Jesus lives out—active peace-making, full of love and care for the least. We are called to show others these unjust realities and invite them to repentance.

Like the crowd, we are also invited to repentance ourselves. John's harsh words could have easily caused the crowd to become defensive, reject John, and leave. Instead, they decided to lean in and be curious; they asked John how they could change. Their response prompts us to question what we do when others call us to repentance. Are we defensive, hardened, and careless? Or are we soft, curious, and open?

Like the crowd, this story is an open invitation to all of us to repent, seek justice, actively care for others, and find Jesus in all of it.

REFLECT

PAUSE   Sit up straight.

Take a deep breath.

Reading the verses today, take a moment to reflect on the story.

PONDER   Invite God to speak to you

I. How often do we hear the call to repent? How do we receive that call? How do we give that call? What does genuine repentance look like?

II. How do our lives reflect the coming Kingdom that John the Baptist was preaching? Can we repent for how they do not?

PRAYER

God of the Coming Kingdom,
may we hear your prophetic words
and turn towards the call to repentance.
May we be baptized and live justly,
making the way for your Way.
Amen.

ASSIGNMENT: Please read 1 Samuel 20 for Lesson Fourteen.

THE STORY OF JONATHAN

Loyalty / Chosen Family
1 Samuel 20

LESSON FOURTEEN

SYNOPSIS   When Jonathan finds himself in a broken family, he seeks the love and loyalty he deserves in David, and the two face challenges as a chosen family.

Read   Jonathan is the eldest son of King Saul, the first king of Israel. As the first-born son, he was born expecting to carry on his father's legacy, but his relationship with his father was rocky. Instead, he found a loyal companion in David, a man secretly anointed to be king of Israel after God rejected Saul as king in God's eyes. David and Jonathan made a covenant—pledging their love and loyalty to each other. Jonathan, the one expected to become king after Saul's death, pledges his loyalty to the newly appointed king even though Saul continued to sit on the throne.

Jonathan finds himself in a complicated relationship with two men who believe they have a claim to the throne. The one Jonathan is related to by blood is careless, angry, and insecure. The one Jonathan is related to by covenant is considered successful, strong, and gentle. Managing these complex relationships in any scenario would have been hard, but so much more difficult once Saul determined he wanted to kill David.

After an attack on his life, David seeks out Jonathan for support and intel as to why Saul wants him dead. Jonathan can't imagine that his father would want to kill David. Though their relationship is rocky, surely Jonathan would have heard about this plot from his father! But David, recalling the recent attempt on his life, guesses Saul knows about their relationship and is intentionally keeping Jonathan in the dark about his plot.

Together, they devise a plan for Jonathan to test Saul's feelings about David. When Jonathan informs Saul that David won't be attending the New Moon festival, Saul flies into a rage, insulting Jonathan, telling him that he knows that Jonathan would rather David be king than himself and sharing his intent to kill David. When Jonathan speaks up on David's behalf, Saul hurls a spear at Jonathan, his firstborn son, in an attempt to kill him.

Crushed by the realization that his father intends to kill his closest companion, Jonathan returns to the place he and David set aside to meet when the plan has been completed. Knowing the only way to save David's life was for him to flee, they tearfully say their goodbyes; it's the last time they ever see each other. Before he goes, Jonathan reaffirms the covenant of loyalty they made before the Lord that bound them and their children together forever.

Years later, Jonathan is killed in battle, and David finally assumes the throne. Searching for any remaining family of

Jonathan's that he can extend kindness to, he discovers that Jonathan's son Mephibosheth is still alive, and out of his loyalty to Jonathan, he gives Mephibosheth Saul's former property and regularly includes him at the king's table.

TODAY Jonathan's story is a story of selflessness, loyalty, and love. It raises the question: Who is our family? Who are we related to by blood? Who are our friends?

What makes a family? Many of us grew up in families that we bonded with and trusted. They cared for us when we were in need and were there for us throughout the twists and turns of life. However, many of us didn't quite have that experience. Maybe we didn't fit in with our families or had a different upbringing. For many of us who grew up without close family ties or safety at home, we had to find other people to be in our corner—whether it be friends, acquaintances, classmates, congregants, or coworkers. No matter who we are or where we come from, we all deserve the unconditional love of a family.

Jonathan's blood family wasn't a safe place for him. He repeatedly fell out of favor with his dad and didn't believe his family had the right to kingship in Israel. But amid his circumstances, he found David—a covenantal companion. They cared for each other, helped, and supported each other through challenging circumstances like family should. They became each other's chosen family in tumultuous times.

For all of us, our close circle will likely change over our lifetimes. Old relationships might become strained, new relationships will become necessary, and our circumstances will always change. What's important is to look for the people who offer the kind of loyalty that David and Jonathan had with each other—the kind of people who have our backs through hard and good times, who will stand up for us as much as they comfort us. Incredible things are possible when we rely on the people who have our best interests at heart.

We, too, can find people who are selfless, loyal, and loving. We, too, can embody those traits and values as we build relationships. Our family will always be our rock from birth for us. But the story of Jonathan is a story that legitimizes all of the chosen families that we've built over our lifetimes. All of our relationships are a gift from God—and maybe the closest and most important relationships will come from the least likely places.

REFLECT

PAUSE   Sit up straight.
                      Take a deep breath.
                      Reading the verses today, take a moment to reflect on the story.

PONDER   Invite God to speak to you

I. What does loyalty mean to you?
II. Who are the people in your life that you consider family, whether you're related by birth or not?
III. How can you nurture your relationships this week?

PRAYER

God of All, thank you to everyone
who has been in my corner throughout my life.
Teach me to be selfless, loyal, and loving.
May I love and be loved by a true friend like I love myself.
Amen.

ASSIGNMENT: Please read 2 Kings Chapters 22 to 23 for Lesson Fifteen.

THE STORY OF JOSIAH

Radical Change
2 Kings 22

LESSON FIFTEEN

SYNOPSIS Josiah faces radical changes in his lifetime as king of Judah—from suddenly becoming king as a child to re-orienting his kingdom as an adult. This story highlights how he responds to these changes and chooses to make change happen for himself and his entire community.

Read Josiah was one of the last kings of Judah before Israel's exile to Babylon. At just eight years old, he was required to change the course of his early life radically by assuming the throne of his father, Amon, after Amon was assassinated by his officials. Elected by "the people of the land," Josiah was suddenly thrust into a position of power, responsibility, and legacy at an impressionable age. While 2 Kings does not offer much insight into Josiah's early childhood, something about his new life trajectory compels him to follow "the example of his ancestor David" and live a life seeking God's will.

At 26 years old, eighteen years into his reign as king, Josiah begins to lean into change—rather than allowing it to be thrust upon him as he did throughout his childhood. While his forebears remain complacent, Josiah desires something different for his kingdom. First, he decides to repair the Temple. He pays carpenters, builders, and masons to help begin the restoration process.

While repairing the Temple, Hilkiah, the high priest, and Shaphan, the secretary, find the Book of the Law. They share it with Josiah. Upon hearing the words of the law, Josiah tears his robes, realizing his lineage has genuinely turned away from God! Immediately, yet again, the trajectory of Josiah's life is at a crossroads. This time, he wholeheartedly embraces change; he renews Judah's covenant with God, tears down all temples, shrines, and altars dedicated to false gods, and reestablishes Israel's generations-old observance of the Passover.

Josiah changed the entire system and society of the kingdom of Judah, and this is greatly acknowledged. The Scripture reflects: "Never before had there been a king like Josia…and there has never been a king like him since."

TODAY As the old adage claims, "the only constant in life is change." We can all recount moments in our past that prompted a radical change in our lives. Perhaps it is the death of a loved one, the birth of a first child, or moving to a new home. These moments shake us out of our current conformities and we are left with a choice: do we embrace the changes happening to us? Or do we try to hold on to old habits, rituals, and ways of life because they feel safe and secure?

Josiah models what a healthy dialogue with change looks like. He experiences radical moments of newness in his life—from his father's death to deciding to repair the temple to discover the Book of the Law—and in each of these moments, he wholeheartedly allows, and even chooses, change. Upon assuming the throne, Josiah could have easily been like his forebears in disregarding the Temple; instead, he sees the need for a change and repairs it. Upon reading the Book of the Law, Josiah could have easily tossed it aside, seeing the necessary changes it prompted as too challenging to accept. Instead, Josiah immediately implements radical changes to the kingdom of Judah, re-establishing it as a kingdom under God.

When we are faced with change, how do we respond?

The story of Josiah invites us to see change as reasonable and necessary. It is an inevitable part of the human experience and offers opportunities for a more prosperous and fuller life and a more fruitful relationship with God.

REFLECT
PAUSE Sit up straight.
Take a deep breath.
Reading the verses today, take a moment to reflect on the story.

PONDER Invite God to speak to you

I. When has radical change altered the shape of your life? How did you respond—with openness or resistance?
II. In what areas do you need to break cycles and choose change, even when it's hard? Where can you choose change for the betterment of the world around you?

PRAYER
Heavenly Father, You are my strength.
With each step with You, my soul is stirred, and my heart sings.
Grant me bravery when I am faced with hardships.
And may I join in the divine melody of life with You. Amen.

ASSIGNMENT: Please read John 11:1-44 for Lesson Sixteen.

THE STORY OF LAZARUS, MARTHA, & MARY

Grief / Hope
John 11:1-44

LESSON SIXTEEN

SYNOPSIS Martha and Mary navigate the delicate balance of hope and grief as they lose their beloved brother, Lazarus.

Read Lazarus and his sisters, Martha and Mary, were from Bethany. The family hosted Jesus in their home during his ministry travels, and Jesus loved them. One day, Lazarus falls ill, and as he begins to deteriorate, the concerned sisters send word to Jesus about their brother's condition. They have seen Jesus' miraculous ability to heal and hope he can do the same for their brother. All of them anxiously wait for Jesus to arrive.

As Lazarus becomes more and more ill, his sisters move from anticipating healing to dreading unimaginable loss. The family is soon struck with tragedy—Lazarus dies. All hope dissipates. What could have been a celebration of his healing becomes a burial for his death as others gather to mourn with the family.

Once Jesus arrives, it's two days too late. Grief is rooted in place as Martha says to Jesus that if he had been there earlier, then their beloved brother would not have died. The cloud of grief casts a shadow on any hope she had of seeing her brother again. She cannot see the promise that stands before her in Jesus— the promise for more than just life after death, but life here and now. She does not fully understand what Jesus means to do, but even in her grief, she chooses to confide in Jesus. Meanwhile, Mary falls at the feet of her Teacher, her Rabbi, as she is anguished over the loss of Lazarus. Both sisters seek the comfort of Jesus in their time of immense sadness, and all of them weep for the death of their brother whom they so loved.

But then Jesus does something that not only pushes the boundaries of belief but also restores the ability to hopefully.

As they approach the tomb, Jesus asks them to remove the stone at the entrance. Martha, with her faith faltering amid grief, tries to stop Jesus by warning him of the odor—Lazarus had already been dead four days! Jesus responds, reminding her that she can experience the glory of God if she holds on to her hope and belief. So, they roll away the stone.

Jesus looks up and gives glory to God, reminding these sisters and the surrounding community that what is about to happen belongs to God. Jesus loudly tells Lazarus, lying lifeless in a tomb, "Lazarus, come out!" He walks out of the tomb. The grief of Lazarus' family transforms into wonder. Those who witnessed the miracle put their faith in Jesus—they experience the glory of God.

TODAY Lazarus's miracle is not about just one person. It includes the story of the people around him and who Jesus is. We see a family concerned, desperate, but hopeful for the miraculous healing they know Jesus can bring. But suddenly, their hope turns to grief after their brother dies. Looking deeper, there is a bittersweet reminder of the intersection of despair and hope.

When we are suddenly met with grief, it can consume us with every breath we take. We are left vulnerable and unable to see the light of tomorrow as the people, the way of life, and the things we wished for suddenly disappear. Financial instability, aging parents, career loss, infertility, political instability, cancer, or long-term illness are all forms of grief we can face today. These experiences may bring a deep sorrow—and even a loss of hope.

Yet, even in heartache, we can be like Martha and Mary and confide in Jesus. We may not fully understand it like them, but we know we can trust Jesus and his promise of life. Even amidst grief, we can allow the faint cracks of hope in Jesus to seep through as we remember he is our ultimate healer.

And, so, the story ends with hopefully restored. Jesus makes death powerless, offering new life, here and now, to Lazarus. Even if it does not take the form of raising a physical body from the dead, we all need this life: the vitality and vividness that makes existing in the world worth it. That is what Jesus offers; he continually asks us to hope, no matter the grief, suffering, and sorrow around us. In a grievous world, do we believe that there is life to be lived on the other side of grief? Can we hope for it?

REFLECT

PAUSE Sit up straight.
Take a deep breath.
Reading the verses today, take a moment to reflect on the story.

PONDER Invite God to speak to you:

I. Have there been times when you have felt consumed by grief, unable to walk through it? What does immovable grief look like?
II. Where can you honestly engage Jesus over these moments of grief? How can you experience greater hope in Jesus amidst this grief?

PRAYER

God of Compassion. I am fragile and in need.
When I am consumed by grief and sorrow overcomes my heart,
walk me from the darkness of death to the vividness of life.
And may all my hope be found in you. Amen.

ASSIGNMENT: Please read Esther Acts 16:11-15 for Lesson Seventeen.

THE STORY OF LYDIA

Hospitality
Acts 16:11-15

LESSON SEVENTEEN

SYNOPSIS As the household leader, Lydia knows she must bring her family and servants to learn about Jesus.

Read Lydia enjoys her regular trips to the riverbank, where a handful of Jews gather to pray. Her work trading purple cloth keeps her busy, successful, and wealthy, but this is one of the places where she can find kindred hearts who seek God.

Today, however, the place of prayer is extra busy. There seem to be some new people, and a man she has never seen before is teaching. The speaker introduces himself as Paul. He and his company traveled from city to city, learning about the Messiah, and God told them to come here to Macedonia.

Paul continues to speak about Jesus Christ, this unexpected servant-king who fulfills all old prophecies and embraces everyone. Lydia hangs on every word. If this good news is true, then it changes everything. The Kingdom of God that Jesus spoke of means that she, this gentile woman and business owner out in Philippi, is someone God loves. She is part of God's home.

As the leader of her household, Lydia knows she must bring her family and servants to learn about this Jesus. That day, she and her whole household are baptized in the river.

But Lydia wants something even more—not just to receive the good news but to participate in it. The good news of the Kingdom of God coming near is more than just a message; welcoming hospitality invites us to see everyone as part of our household.

Using her resources as a purple cloth dealer, she offers to host Paul and his company for as long as they like. Being associated with a traveling preacher like Paul will reflect on her social standing and clientele, but she can't help it—the good news changes her.

TODAY God's good news is one of hospitality—a warm embrace extended to everyone, even those with unique intersectional identities. Lydia is one of these individuals; she is a gentile, a worshiper of God, a business owner, a woman, a head of the household, and a wealthy person. This amalgamation of identities is uncommon in the first century CE. But the good news welcomes her as it does to all.

What do we do when met with such a powerful, hospitable force? We welcome others into it! Lydia first shows hospitality to the rest of her household; she does not hold this good news to herself but invites them all to experience it. And then she goes further; she understands this good news of hospitality means her household, her family, has grown—Paul and his companions are also part of that household. She uses her unique identity and resources and warmly welcomes them into her home.

Hospitality is at the core of the Gospel message. It is an enclosing air that enfolds us with all good things: love, belonging, coziness, kindness, and affection. Like Lydia's, the natural response to this experience is to bring about hospitality ourselves—to share generously, no matter how big or small, invite others into our homes, and use our unique identities to show our distinctive neighborliness. Who can we welcome today?

REFLECT

PAUSE Sit up straight.
Take a deep breath.
Reading the verses today, take a moment to reflect on the story.

PONDER Invite God to speak to you:

I. How do you see God's good news as an expression of hospitality?
II. How have you experienced hospitality from others? Please take a moment to express gratitude for their generosity.
III. Where can you uniquely share generosity and hospitality with others?

PRAYER

God, thank you for the divine example of hospitality.
Thank you for the home you have opened to me
through the Gospel message you bring.
Teach me to live with open doors for my many siblings in
Christ. Amen

ASSIGNMENT: Please read John 9 for Lesson Eighteen.

THE STORY OF THE MAN BORN BLIND

Shame / Discernment
John 9

LESSON EIGHTEEN

SYNOPSIS A man born blind is miraculously healed. His healing restores his humanity away from shame and towards a newfound faith and belonging.

Read Our story opens with Jesus' disciples asking about a man who has been blind from birth. Their questioning shows a common assumption of that period—sickness and disability are caused by sin—an assumption that this man had grown up with, hanging over his very existence.

Jesus' disciples assume that someone must have sinned for the man to have been born blind, but who can know? Perhaps he committed some heinous act in the womb, or his parents had sinned in such a way as to be punished with a blind child. Such whispered judgments were familiar rhetoric as the man got older. When everyone around you assumes you or your family have earned God's punishment, shame and isolation encroach on your identity.

Undermining these assumptions, Jesus responds with a different viewpoint—man's blindness isn't an indication of God's curse but an opportunity for God's power to be seen in him. How would he choose to display this?

He spits on the ground. Mixing his saliva with dirt, he creates a muddy concoction and puts it on the man's eyes.

Jesus directs the man, "Go, wash in the Pool of Siloam," and moves along the path.

Upon washing, the man's eyes were opened. Who realized this healing? The mud had covered his ability to see the healer's face before he had left.

While the man is rejoicing, his neighbors, the same ones who had known him as a blind beggar, have trouble recognizing him. It could be because of his physical healing, but this man had also experienced emotional and social healing, replacing his shame with confidence and belonging.

His transformation leads to a disagreement among the people, which brings him to the Pharisees to settle the dispute. The questioning turns into an interrogation when the Pharisees realize the healing took place on the Sabbath, and the focus shifts from the healed man to the person who brought the healing.

"I think he must be a prophet," the man says.

Unhappy with the situation, the Pharisees bring in the man's parents as character witnesses, but their quick responses absolve themselves from the controversy surrounding their son.

The Pharisees return to questioning the man a second time. Frustrated by their disbelief, the man states that God only listens to those who do God's will. Only God could have the power to heal someone born blind. Perhaps the man is encouraged by his new status in society as a seeing man; however, in any case, his arguments anger the Pharisees. Enraged, they fire back with their underlying assumption: that the man's disability had been caused by his sinfulness. They throw him out of the synagogue.

Hearing about the encounter, Jesus seeks out the man he healed and reveals himself as the one who had healed him. Immediately, the man puts his belief in Jesus and worships him as Lord.

Jesus commends him for his discernment and ends the story with a warning to anyone who claims to see but cannot see Jesus for who he truly is. In the end, it seems the Pharisees were the ones who were truly blind.

TODAY We can see from the Man Born Blind's story that shame and judgment are designed to keep us down and alone. As social scientist Brené Brown describes, "Shame corrodes the very part of us that believes we are capable of change." This man had grown up with the weight of the belief that his very existence was proof of God's displeasure and punishment. Not only was he navigating life with a disability, he was living as a pariah in his town, isolated and condemned. The only option for his future was to accept pity and scorn as a beggar. We, too, may feel the destructive realities of shame and long to be free from its power. Shame creeps in when we feel like imposters in professional settings, replay past rejections and mistakes in our heads, or compare our lives to others whom we perceive to be more likable.

In restoring the man's physical sight, Jesus reaches through his wall of shame, dignifies him in front of his community, and, as a result, leads the man to a deeper faith, which is displayed to those around him.

When our humanity is restored, it can lead to greater faith. In this story, greater faith is created in more than just a singular moment of physical healing— but rather a conscious recalibration of the man's entire life in light of that healing. For his whole life, such a public argument with the Pharisees would have been treated with disdain. Yet, as displayed by his boldness to respond publicly to his accusers, he embodies an imaginative model of faith accessible to anyone marginalized through shame. It is a much-needed antidote for a corroded world.

The story of the man born blind reminds us that Jesus' healing is multifaceted. Not only does Jesus heal bodies, but he also heals our relationships with ourselves and the world around us. For those who experience shame, Jesus invites our muddy eyes to experience a renewed life.

REFLECT

PAUSE   Sit up straight.

Take a deep breath.

Reading the verses today, take a moment to reflect on the story.

PONDER   Invite God to speak to you:

I. Are there areas in your life where you feel shame?
II. In what areas have you lost the belief that you are capable of change? What would it take to grow that belief?
III. Where have you experienced healing? In what ways are you invited to live in light of that healing?

PRAYER

To the God who sees what is deeply rooted in my heart;
who feels the shame we have hidden within us;
we pray that you may make me whole
when shame corrodes my being.
Amen.

ASSIGNMENT: Please read Exodus 2:1-10 for Lesson Nineteen.

THE STORY OF MIRIAM

Watchfulness / Survival
Exodus 2:1-10

LESSON NINETEEN

SYNOPSIS   Miriam watches over Moses and the future of Israel, participating in the cooperative task of their survival.

Read   Exodus 2 recounts the story of a group of women who thwart Pharaoh's plans and save the Hebrew child, Moses, who would go on to save the Hebrew people. A Levite couple has Moses, and seeing that the child is good, beautiful, and healthy, the mother hides the child, defying Pharaoh's order that every Hebrew boy should be killed by being thrown into the Nile.1 Pharaoh miscalculates and thinks the Hebrew men threaten his rule2, but the women defy him. In Exodus 1, two midwives reject Pharaoh's command to kill the Hebrew boys. In Exodus 2, Moses' mother, sister, Pharaoh's daughter, and Pharaoh's maid refuse to obey Pharaoh and become the saviors of the Hebrew people.

When she could no longer hide Moses, his mother, Jochebed3, created an ark to place Moses in the Nile River. Cleverly, Jochebed found a way to "obey" Pharaoh's word, putting her son in the river while disobeying him and saving her baby. Jochebed tricks Pharaoh. Her story exemplifies the trickster motif of the Ancient Near Eastern world, where those with less power find creative ways to trick the powerful. Exodus 2 views Jochebed's trickery favorably—it is even salvific!

After Moses is set on the water, his sister, Miriam, watches him to see what will happen. We can wonder what leads Miriam to this. Perhaps after corralling the courage to initiate the plan, Jochebed can no longer watch, but Miriam cannot keep her eyes off of her brother. She takes it upon herself to become her brother's keeper and to be concerned for his life.

And fortunately, Miriam does watch. Pharaoh's daughter sees the baby floating amidst the reeds and sends her maid to bring it. Pharaoh's daughter, knowing this is a Hebrew child and knowing her father has commanded the death of Hebrew children, is still moved to pity the baby. Miriam does not wait. She sees her moment and quickly devises a plan. Perhaps Miriam is already operating with the inspiration of God, which is acknowledged when she is later named as one of the few female prophets of the Hebrew Bible. She makes herself known and speaks up to royalty, suggesting she find a Hebrew woman to nurse the baby for her. Pharaoh's daughter agrees, not knowing the baby will return to his mother.

This is the first time Miriam stands beside the waters to witness liberation.

Later, in Exodus 15, Miriam again stands beside the waters of the Reed Sea. The water parts for the Israelites, but the Egyptians, driven by Pharaoh's violent desire to keep the Hebrew people enslaved, follow and are defeated as the waters close in on them. This Pharaoh's father had previously tried to use the life-giving waters of the Nile as a vehicle for death, but here it is as if the waters have turned back on Pharaoh himself. The people of Israel experience liberation.

At the water's edge, Miriam takes a tambourine and invites all the Hebrew people to join her in a song of praise to YHWH. "Sing to YHWH" is an imperative phrase. As a prophet, Miriam takes up her authority over all the people of Israel—the young, the old, and all genders. It is widely agreed that Miriam's song is one of the oldest texts of the Hebrew Bible. The Song of the Sea, sung by Moses in Exodus 15:1-18 is likely an expansion on Miriam's song. Miriam, who witnesses the birth of her brother and watches over him, is also the prophetic witness of the birth of Israel through the waters. By the time of the New Testament, we can see Miriam's name has become revered among the Jewish people. It is even the name of Jesus' mother. English translations obscure this by translating the Greek Mariám as Mary. Still, she is another Miriam called by YHWH, who witnesses the birth of a savior and prophetically sings God's praises at the advent of YHWH's salvation.

TODAY In Exodus 2, we witness the clever cooperation of the disempowered who struggle towards survival. There is much to learn here. Survival is not an individual task but a cooperative task. It also requires that we can see, evaluate, and sometimes reject authorities that oppose well-being, even tricking the powerful into preserving life. Several commentators have noticed that Moses' birth is a story of internal migration. It resonates with the experiences of migrant peoples who take on extreme risks and defy political structures to survive.

Part of our task, like Miriam's, is to remain watchful. We must see how it goes with our family, neighbors, and the vulnerable.

We must remain attentive and ready. This is indeed part of Miriam's prophetic task. This watchfulness brings about the opportunity for intervention. It also brings about the chance to witness liberation—like the saving of baby Moses—happen all around us.

The prophetic task we are called to is to celebrate liberation and invite others into that celebration. In Exodus 15, as the Reed Sea washes away Pharaoh's army, the people of Israel experience profound liberation. Miriam sees this and does not hold it to herself—she invites her people to sing! It is part of the prophetic task to see when people are set free from the variety of oppressions and enslavements they face, not to let the moment pass quietly or even with individual satisfaction, but to call everyone to praise and celebration.

MORE THAN WORDS

REFLECT
PAUSE   Sit up straight.
Take a deep breath.
Reading the verses today, take a moment to reflect on the story.
PONDER   Invite God to speak to you

I. How can we remain watchful on behalf of the people in our lives who are in need?
II. How have you participated in the survival of goodness in our world?
III. How have you celebrated with the community when people are set free from oppression?

PRAYER
Heavenly Father, give us that discernment
to see the people in our lives who are in need.
We pray that we shall be intentional in our watchfulness on
the needs of others
rather than focus on our own struggles in life.
There are more people out there who need our help.
Lead us to them, and use us to give them
the blessings that you wish to shower upon them. Amen.

ASSIGNMENT: Please read 2 Kings 5:1-19 for Lesson Twenty

THE STORY OF NAAMAN

Openness / Counsel from Unexpected Places
2 Kings 5:1-19

LESSON TWENTY

SYNOPSIS In an era when Aram caused great affliction to the Israelites, a military commander named Naaman was physically healed by the prophet Elisha. Along his journey, he discovers the power of openness and finds counsel in unexpected places.

Read While the Israelites were in continual conflict with the kingdom of Aram, 2 Kings 5 accounts an unusual story of healing. Naaman was a man who held great power as a leader in the Aramean army, surrounded by respect and fear. Yet, he was plagued with a skin disease that would have caused him both physical and social distress.

In this context, Naaman hears from a young Israelite servant about a person who could heal him: the Israelite prophet Elisha. Naaman could have easily disregarded this information. First, the information comes from a captured servant—a source not likely to be taken seriously because of their low place in society. Second, the information comes from an Israelite—with whom the Arameans have intense conflict.

Despite this, Naaman, out of desperation, chooses to be open to the possibility of healing. He asks the King of Aram for permission to leave for Israel and find Elisha.

A letter travels ahead of Naaman to the King of Israel as a means of peace. Upon receiving the letter, the King of Israel is distraught, mistaking Naaman's travel as potentially hostile. The prophet Elisha hears of the king's distress. Elisha sends the King of Israel a message to have Naaman sent to his home to be healed and experience God's power.

But as Naaman arrives, he is not greeted by Elisha but by Elisha's servant, Gehazi. The servant Gehazi instructs Naaman to wash in the Jordan River seven times to receive complete healing and restoration.

Why had Naaman not received more respect and been greeted by the prophet rather than this servant? Couldn't Elisha wave his hand and call the name of God to give Naaman immediate healing? What was the difference between bathing in the Jordan River and the rivers back in Syria?

Naaman's servants, listening to his confusion and anger, remind him: wouldn't complete healing be worth seven dips in the Jordan River as unbelievable as it seemed? Naaman, in his rage, seems poised to ignore Elisha's instructions—but again, in his desperation, he chooses to be open to the possibility of healing. Naaman, emotionally raw and hopeful, goes down to the Jordan and follows the instructions of God's prophet. After the seventh bath, Naaman's skin is completely healed; he is finally cleansed.

Amazed, Naaman returns to Elisha's house to offer gratitude for his healing, proclaiming that there is no god other than the God of Israel. Elisha sends Naaman off with a blessing of peace.

TODAY Naaman was an influential military leader likelier to command and order others than listen to them. He could have easily ignored the suggestions of the Israelite servant girl, Gehazi, or his servants. Still, Naaman chose hope instead of openness and desperation and listened to them. As a result, he was healed.

When we look at our culture today, we are often asked if we possess the same level of openness as Naaman. How frequently do we change our minds? How are we usually open to other people, especially those with less social status than us? Do we believe that God is in those people? Do we believe healing can come from unexpected places?

Our culture entices us to listen only to the powerful, noteworthy, and familiar. But the story of Naaman reminds us that God's counsel and instructions can often come from those whom society would deem lacking a voice worth listening to.

Like Naaman, we could be better. When offered something different from our expectations, we may quickly become frustrated or close-minded. But Naaman invites us to let go of rigid expectations and be open to the possibility of something new—even healing. Are we open and attentive?

REFLECT

PAUSE — Sit up straight.
Take a deep breath.
Reading the verses today, take a moment to reflect on the story.

PONDER — Invite God to speak to you

I. Are there areas in your life that require healing?
II. Who do you go to in times of need? Can you expand your community and listen to counsel from unexpected places?
III. How open-minded are you when presented with something different from your expectations?

PRAYER

Heavenly Father, you are the God who heals,
I pray that You teach me to find counsel
in unexpected places.
Please help me be open to new possibilities,
ways of living, and healing. Amen.

ASSIGNMENT: Please read Ruth Chapter 1 for Lesson Twenty-One.

CHAPTER 21

THE STORY OF NAOMI

Loss / Community
Ruth 1

LESSON TWENTY-ONE

SYNOPSIS   Naomi's story is about loss, what it means to pick up the pieces amidst grief, and how to invite the community into our experience.

Read   As the Book of Ruth opens, Naomi loses her homeland. There is a famine in Bethlehem of Judah, so Naomi, her husband, and their two sons leave the land they have always known and settle in Moab. There, her husband dies, leaving Naomi with her two sons in a foreign land. As they settle there, each son marries a local woman. Ten years later, the unthinkable happens, and both Naomi's sons die. A parent losing a child is a uniquely deep grief, and Naomi experiences it twofold.

Naomi is without a homeland, a husband, and no children. Her life is gutted by loss.

But her loss doesn't happen in a vacuum. Naomi has two daughters-in-law, Orpah and Ruth. And they hear some good news—that God has once again blessed Naomi's homeland with good crops, so she and her daughters-in-law can begin to make their way there.

Except.

Realizing these young women still have many years where they might raise children with new husbands, Naomi implores them to go back to Moab to their families, their gods, and their way of life. They have lost their husbands, yet their story is not over. Naomi, on the other hand, feels her age. She will have no more children. She feels the heaviness of all the losses she has endured over the years, one after another, and through it, all senses God's fist raised against her. This is not simply a series of painful life events; for Naomi, it holds deep spiritual significance. It shows that her God is not protecting her. She knows that God holds the world, and her world has fallen apart. She feels God is against her.

They weep together, and Orpah returns to her family.

But not Ruth. Ruth refuses to leave.

No matter how much Naomi pleads with her, Ruth remains. This decision means significant losses for Ruth—her homeland, family, and gods. But while Naomi's losses are out of her control, Ruth chooses these losses. For Ruth, not remaining with Naomi would be the most significant loss. She commits to making Naomi's land, people, and God her own, and they journey toward Bethlehem together.

When Naomi returns to her homeland, the people she had left so many years before welcome her back. But she needs them to know she's changed. *Naomi* means "pleasant." And she is not the Naomi they learned years ago, with a loving husband, two healthy sons, and a sense of God's benevolence toward her. Instead, she is bitter, empty, and has endured great suffering, and she needs her kindred to understand this. So, she insists they call her by a new name, *Mara,* "bitterness," so they will all have to acknowledge, every time they speak of her, the deep loss that God has brought into her life.

TODAY As we think about the losses we have experienced; we may notice how they felt different depending on whether they were something we chose or something thrust upon us.

Losses like deciding to end a relationship, moving to a new city, or changing jobs are similar to Ruth's. Though they contain the pain of loss, we also have a sense of choice and control. But other kinds of loss, like a complex medical diagnosis, the death of a loved one, or being let go from a job, are losses similarly experienced by Naomi. These losses shatter us to our core precisely because they are uncontrollable, turbulent, and confusing.

In seasons when losses feel thrust upon us, like Naomi's, we might experience God as being against us, sending tragedies into our lives. Naomi doesn't feel the need to rescue God's reputation or qualify her experience of God with "right theology." Instead, she is honest and unflinching about her spiritual life after shattering losses. Do we feel such freedom when feeling far from God—why or why not?

Naomi even gives herself a new name, calling her community to see her and acknowledge her pain. She invites us to wonder how seriously we take our places of pain and loss. Do we invite the people around us to see us in our pain and hold it with us? What name do we ask people to call us?

REFLECT

PAUSE Sit up straight.
Take a deep breath.
Reading the verses today, take a moment to reflect on the story.

PONDER Invite God to speak to you

I. In what areas of your life do you want to express more honestly (whether with God, yourself, or others)?
II. Are there situations of pain in your own story you haven't yet acknowledged? What would it look like to grieve these situations and invite the community to support you?

PRAYER

God of Comfort and Sovereignty,
when I set out whole and am brought back empty with loss,
lend me the courage to be honest within. In grief,
may I turn my heart to you and my community
and return help to loved ones in pain,
where wholeness is found. Amen.

ASSIGNMENT: Please read Nehemiah Chapters 1 & 2 for Lesson Twenty-Two.

THE STORY OF NEHEMIAH

Going to God for Repair
Nehemiah 1-2

LESSON TWENTY-TWO

SYNOPSIS Nehemiah journeys from his place in King Artaxerxes' court to his broken homeland, awaiting God's timing with wisdom, faith, and slowness. God makes a way for Nehemiah's participation and restoration.

Read Born in Persia to parents exiled from Jerusalem, Nehemiah ascended to a place of prominence in King Artaxerxes' court as his cup-bearer. In this position, Nehemiah was highly trusted and would ensure the king and his guests had ample (unpoisoned) wine throughout their gatherings.

Nehemiah receives news that in Jerusalem, the homeland of his parents, the city's walls have been torn down and its gates burned. Jerusalem's strong walls enabled it to thrive and for its people to flourish and dwell in more excellent safety. It is now in ruins. Nehemiah is devastated.

For many days, he slows down and intentionally takes time to hold this news in his heart and before God. Mourning, fasting, and praying, Nehemiah beseeches God to look favorably on the people of Judah and begins to wonder whether his relationship with the king might open a way for Nehemiah himself to intervene.

Still grieving Jerusalem's brokenness, he cannot hide his sorrow when Nehemiah comes to serve the king that spring. King Artaxerxes notices and asks about it.

Nehemiah laments that the land where his ancestors are buried is in shambles.

The king asks what he can do to help.

Recognizing God's movement in this moment, Nehemiah knows this is not a time for timidity. He prays for God to work through this conversation and tells the king that he wants to travel to Judah to rebuild the city.

This is no small trip. Jerusalem is more than 1,000 miles from Persia, and Nehemiah knows he'll need protection as he travels and supplies to rebuild the city's walls when he arrives. He boldly asks what he needs for the repair work on his heart. The king grants all of Nehemiah's requests, which Nehemiah knows is due to God's loving intervention.

After a long journey, Nehemiah arrives in Jerusalem.

Just as Nehemiah had a slow inwardness with God before creating a plan to share with the king, Nehemiah slows down and proceeds with deliberate, prayerful intentionality. Initially, he holds to his plans to rebuild the wall only within his own heart. With a small group of men, he surveys the tragic ruins of the city and takes time to let his plans and feelings percolate.

Finally, he tells the city officials and religious leaders what he has come to Jerusalem to do.

As he tells the Jewish leaders of his plan, he relies not merely on his passion and charisma to persuade them but emphasizes that God has provided for him and opened the way for this to happen all along the way. They joyfully welcome his plan.

Some city officials mock him scornfully, but Nehemiah remains steadfast despite their derision. He reiterates his plans to rebuild the wall, knowing that "The God of heaven will help us succeed."

TODAY When a situation of brokenness grieves us, how quickly do we respond? And how much do we trust God to make way for restoration?

We might notice something that needs healing on a grand scale, like Nehemiah's project for the welfare of a whole city. Alternatively, it might be on a smaller scale, like bringing a new form of care and justice into our neighborhood, for God's healing to enter a longstanding dynamic in our family, or for something that needs repair in our hearts.

Nehemiah's deliberate and prayerful slowness invites us to reflect on our own pace of engaging with God about the places around and within us that need repair—no matter how daunting. It reminds us that God is the one who will make a way.

When we notice something is broken, we may feel overwhelmed and find it difficult to respond or act. On the other hand, in a hurried society, we might respond with immediate action to gain a sense of false control over the situation.

Nehemiah shows us another way. He does act (which is crucial!), but it's surrounded by prayer, slowness, and intentionality. Each step along the way includes him paying attention to his own feelings, his surroundings, and, maybe most importantly, how God is showing up. His persistent trust in God enables his slowness, and God responds in partnership with Nehemiah. What seemed like an overwhelming task is possible because God is forging a path forward.

What would it look like to respond to the brokenness we notice in our lives and our world with the deliberate slowness and persistent trust that Nehemiah has? Could we also ground ourselves in prayer, make space for feelings of pain and grief, and remain attentive to God's power and movement? Could we trust God to work with us towards restoration?

MORE THAN WORDS

REFLECT
PAUSE Sit up straight.
Take a deep breath.
Reading the verses today, take a moment to reflect on the story.
PONDER Invite God to speak to you

I. What was a time when you rushed in to fix a problem without spending time with yourself and with God first? What might you have done differently if you had brought the issue to God before acting?
II. Do you have a story in which God made even the most unlikely or surprisingly practical aspects come into place for goodness to be done?
III. How can we be more sensitive to when God is doing more than we know so we can attentively wait for our time to participate in restoration?

PRAYER
O God of restoration, may I see your way being made
behind the scenes and in the unexpected things.
When should I be slow and allow you to set me up
to participate in making the world whole? Amen.

ASSIGNMENT: Please read Philemon Chapter 1 for Lesson Twenty-Three.

THE STORY OF ONESIMUS

Liberation & Freedom
Philemon 1

LESSON TWENTY THREE

SYNOPSIS In this chapter, we contemplate how the Gospel story could stir Onesimus to chase freedom from slavery in the face of institutionalized oppressive power.

Read The story of Onesimus's journey to freedom is laid out in an advocacy letter from Paul to Onesimus's former master, Philemon. Onesimus was Philemon's slave—until he freed himself and escaped the bonds of slavery. Paul writes on his behalf, vouching for Onesimus to be received by Philemon with peace, not as a slave once again, but as a free man who would be considered an equal. Issues of power, honor, dignity, and agency are all on the table, and the good news of Christ and the Kingdom of God spread throughout the Mediterranean. The Roman-ruled society of the time rests on the idea that slaves, women, and children are all effectively disposable. So, the freedom of one slave would be a threat to the whole of Roman society, which makes Onesimus' self-emancipation so problematic to those in power.

Let's imagine where the idea of freedom takes root for Onesimus. What kind of story from what kind of people could subvert the realities of Roman society and allow Onesimus to believe in the possibility of freedom?

It is sparked by the counter-cultural story that Christ has come and risen! And it is the knowledge that this story of Christ is connected to the liberating stories of Yahweh—which has resonated in the bones of Jewish people for generations: Yahweh, the one who freed people from slavery in Egypt. Yahweh, the God Hagar, is named in Genesis. Yahweh, who sees and cares for the vulnerable. It is against the backdrop of Yahweh as a liberator and the rumors of a Rabbi claiming to be the Son of Yahweh for everyone that allows slaves like Onesimus to imagine a life filled with freedom and hope.

Day after day, Onesimus tends to his slave duties with a growing imagination for his freedom and self-worth, bothering him like a rock in his shoe. The good news that this inclusive God has finally come back agitates him as he tries to continue the everyday routines of his life. The hopeful thought of liberty disrupts his ability to continue living in the reality of being a slave. Yahweh

is the God who liberates the powerless, and Christ has come to set the captives free!

He hears more and more about Jesus, the new Rabbi who claims to be The Anointed One and of whom the Jewish community has been waiting for ultimate liberation. Imagine fellow slaves sharing bits and pieces of Jesus' teachings that snap Onesimus from a submissive, subservient image of himself and give him imagination for freedom—a new reality of being a child of

God. This liberating narrative of including those who are culturally considered the least honorable in the family of God undermines all the stories and systems that keep Onesimus a slave. With a new image of himself as a child of God, there is no way he can participate in someone else's flourishing at the expense of his own. Inspired by a new sense of identity in Christ, he takes new steps in faith, each step away from slavery and toward an identity centered on being cherished by God.

TODAY Onesimus embodies the liberation made possible by trusting our hearts, encounters with God, and divine imagination. Onesimus' story can remind us of individuals like Dr. Martin Luther King Jr., who made his home in Alabama during the heart of severe Anti-Blackness in the late 50s, to realize a reality only vivid in his imagination. A reality where "little black girls and boys are playing with little white girls and boys" without the violence of racism. There was a yearning in the hearts of Black folks to experience the liberation and flourishing life God intends for everyone—to fully enter into the freedom and unity of the good news. Dr. King took very courageous steps to swim upstream, along with all his contemporaries, against the systemic oppression of his people. They marched against the flow of theological interpretation and cultural norms of the time to live in a new image of freedom.

Onesimus and Dr. King invite us to take our encounters with God and the promises of God's Kingdom seriously. Jesus invites us to liberation in every way we need it! The transformative, life-giving freedom of the Gospel is for us all in this present moment of our lives. Many of us have been part of institutions or communities that explicitly or implicitly made us suppress personal truths and forms of identity honored by God. Onesimus gives us a picture of what it looks like to courageously take steps away from those places of oppression and move toward liberation.

Onesimus' liberation started with good news, completely disrupting his reality and provoking him to imagine a new way of being. It reminds us of the same good news—we are all cherished children of God. There are days when every sense of powerlessness and wound in our lives is outshined by new realities of belovedness and a constellation of relationships that remind us just how cherished we are. Our journey to complete healing and hope begins with one faithful step to honor our hearts as we follow the compelling voice of Christ calling us toward freedom.

MORE THAN WORDS

REFLECT

PAUSE   Sit up straight.

Take a deep breath.

Reading the verses today, take a moment to reflect on the story.

PONDER   Invite God to speak to you

I. How do you think Onesimus felt with a newfound sense of identity walking into the same kinds of relationships and institutions that led to his oppression?

II. Can you name realities, relationships, people, and systems that make you feel like a prisoner to an identity that is less than a cherished child of God? How would you describe a reality where you are entirely liberated?

III. Have you ever had to break conventional wisdom, believing there had to be more for you? What did it cost you? Was the freedom worth the cost?

IV. When do you feel most free? Who makes you feel most free? What hobbies help you to be your most liberated self? How can you do more of that in your life?

PRAYER

God of freedom, please help me ignite our divine imagination to make absolute subversive freedom
in dark times for ourselves and the world. Amen.

ASSIGNMENT: Please read Acts Chapter 10 for Lesson Twenty-Four.

CHAPTER 24

THE STORY OF PETER & CORNELIUS

Unexpected Gatherings
Acts 10

LESSON TWENTY-FOUR

SYNOPSIS   Through their shared love of God, Peter and Cornelius, Jew and Gentile, discover an unexpected kinship and purpose with one another.

Read   We begin with Cornelius. As a centurion of the superpower Rome, he has political privilege, military prowess, and impressive wealth. Despite his lofty status, Cornelius is portrayed as someone who yearns for God and loves God's people. But in the Jews' eyes, he is a Gentile: a term used to describe the people whose ethnic, cultural, and spiritual status placed them outside of the bounds of being God's family. Ironically, Cornelius is

| 117 |

on the outside and wants to belong to God's family. Contrary to Jew-Gentile constructs, however, God is aware of Cornelius' presence. God sees Cornelius' love for others and God and wants to bring Cornelius into the Divine family. But to do this, God directs Cornelius to seek a kind of person he does not expect—a Jew.

We meet Peter in his prayers and hunger during fasting— a practice linked to religious communities for millennia. Speaking to one of his needs, God calls on Peter to kill and eat. Peter refuses because many of these animals are "unclean, impure" for a Jew to consume according to Jewish Law. Only Gentiles like Cornelius—those that Jews perceive as not belonging to God's family— eat these things. Peter's need to remain religiously faithful and nourish himself are opposed to each other, but in God's eyes, they are not. God suggests something far more radical to Peter than to get hung up on outdated, legalistic frameworks. These animals represented the world and life of the Gentiles, so eating these animals was to enmesh oneself with other people. Peter, however, struggles to accept this. He is unable to sense God's new work of inclusion and embrace. God is turning Peter in his prayer and hunger, not toward God's self per se, but to a kind of person Peter doesn't expect to need—a Gentile.

Eventually, the two who were never supposed to meet came face to face. Despite being unsure why they are in each other's company, they both seek to listen to each other earnestly. As Cornelius speaks genuinely, Peter understands that God does not show favoritism but accepts people from every nation.

As Peter has done, he narrates Jesus's radical, inclusive love, which embraces all and condemns oppressive powers, a love that not even threat and death can break.

But before Peter can finish telling his story, God intervenes. The same Spirit that brought God's loving, inclusive presence into the lives of all Jews now embraces Gentiles. Peter and Cornelius, Jew and Gentile, share in the same love of God—who sees them both as family. God transforms their need to be close to God to need life with *each other*. The story of Cornelius and Peter reverberates throughout the rest of history, challenging the faith's understanding of who God calls family, who we will find God working within, and who we call sister, brother, and sibling.

TODAY In our intensely polarized society, it is hard to envision a gathering between two radically different people, let alone imagine them calling each other siblings. We, however, cannot forget how unexpected and inconceivable the meeting between Cornelius and Peter was for everyone at the time. The meeting was so unlikely that God needed to build toward it over time—and we can still glean wisdom from their journeys today.

God first prepares Cornelius' and Peters' hearts to meet someone unexpected; God comes to both of them in visions, laying the foundation for their eventual encounter. Then, when they finally do meet, Cornelius and Peter choose to *genuinely listen* to each other despite their different contexts and cultures. They are curious and ask questions of one another: "May I ask why you have sent me?" And finally, both individuals loved and cherished God wholeheartedly and chose to trust that reality in one another. God's Spirit is revealed only after these things, and an unexpected community is formed.

Maybe that is where we all can start: finding people of faith across race, gender, sexual orientation, class, etc., ready to listen to the other because of a shared love for the Divine. Maybe we, too, need inner preparatory work to understand why it is difficult to believe God is at work in the other. The unexpected gathering cannot be forced, and it isn't instantaneous. It needs Divine power and must be built on listening and trust. These initial steps, however, can make a required bridge toward the other who God already sees as family.

REFLECT
PAUSE Sit up straight.
Take a deep breath.
Reading the verses today, take a moment to reflect on the story.
PONDER Invite God to speak to you

I. What faith stories have you grown up with that teach you to call people unclean and impure? Where do those stories come from? How does this story speak to those stories you have heard?
II. Who is the other in your neighborhood; in your family? What would it mean to listen to the Divine in their story? How could you start building that bridge of trust, humility, and bravery toward them?

PRAYER
God, who loves us as we are, where we are,
and who shares the Spirit generously,
please generate in us the ability to see you at work
in each other's life.
Guide each other to live together
at the table of your Presence. Amen.

ASSIGNMENT: Please read Ecclesiastes 2 for Lesson Twenty-Five.

THE STORY OF THE PREACHER

Futility / MMeaning of Life
Ecclesiastes 2

LESSON TWENTY-FIVE

SYNOPSIS This narrative explains the meaning of life—or rather, what it isn't. The Preacher has explored every avenue of life, shared his wisdom, and invited us to consider what we should and should not pursue.

Read The wisdom of Ecclesiastes singes like white charcoal. The unrelenting words of Qoheleth, or the Preacher, reduce to ashes both simple optimism and strict life principles. Nothing escapes his searing criticisms. Everything is *hevel*—vanity, meaningless, wisps of smoke.

The contested identity of the Preacher (whether Solomon or a different wisdom figure) is not nearly as important as his fiery polemic. He captures the crux of his rant with a guttural cry: Everything is *hevel*, utterly *hevel*. Commonly translated as "meaningless" or "vanity," *hevel* is much more nebulous than that. The best translation is also its best imagery: wisps of smoke. *Hevel* is fleeting and impossible to grasp. Likewise, the Preacher concludes that life is short and the meaning of life is always shrouded in smoke—a constant enigma. Even the surest things in life lose clarity and stability in this smoke.

In Ecclesiastes 2, the Preacher focuses on three life pillars: pleasure, wisdom, and work. He has summited the pinnacles of life. He has experienced heights very few can identify with, and most would toil relentlessly to taste. Nonetheless, he recounts his life in a way the unfortunate and weary find familiar: Everything is *hevel,* utterly *hevel*.

The Preacher has savored pleasure in all its forms: large estates, enviable gardens, slaves and servants, vast flocks, immense riches, endless entertainment, coveted concubines, and satisfaction from his labors. When these were not enough, he amassed more— nothing was denied. He became the greatest in Jerusalem, adored and envied. Nevertheless, he concludes nothing was worthwhile. Pleasure is *hevel.*

The Preacher has experienced great wisdom but stifles any optimism bent toward it. The wise and the fool will share the same fate; both will die. What, then, is the value of wisdom? Furthermore, both sages and fools will be forgotten in the grand scheme of time. The universe does not care whether one life is wise or foolish. Long before us, the sun rose from the east; long after us, the sun will still set in the west—wholly unphased by the death of one life. Wisdom is hevel.

Finally, the Preacher finds much success in work—but, too, says it is futile. The strivings, triumphs, failures, and regrets are in vain. We take none to the grave. Sleepless nights plagued with worries, debilitating years of anxiety, and a long and arduous life—where is the value when everyone will return to dust? Even if we pass the fruits of our labors to our successors, who knows what will happen to our fortunes and their lives? The rich and the poor, the successful and the failures, are equal before death. Success is hevel.

And, so, the Preacher chases after every human desire imaginable. But ultimately, he concludes that chasing after these things—pleasure or wisdom or work—is meaningless, akin to chasing after the wind.

TODAY Vanity of vanities! Everything is meaningless! Nothing matters!

The Preacher seems to scrape the depths of today's buried, ejected cries. How often do we try to fulfill ourselves with luxurious pleasures only to find they fall short? After experiencing incredible success, how often do we crave even more success—realizing the goalposts are constantly moving? Life seems so futile before these harsh realities. They thwart our hopes and the ability to dream. Amid these hurricanes and more, it is appropriate and understandable first to read the Preacher's words as a fiery nihilism. But alongside that nihilism, there's another truth simmering beneath the surface. The Preacher looks straight into the eyes of our deepest human cravings, the things that feel so vitally important, and he calls them hevel. The Preacher is doing us a favor. He has reached the apex of human possibility in pleasure, wisdom, and work but concludes they are all futile. He has gone before us, so we don't have to; we are invited to let go of our struggles and strife—knowing these endeavors are meaningless.

Wisdom can come from many sources. In the Bible, books like Proverbs and Ecclesiastes offer wisdom from different perspectives. Wisdom, from any source, invites us to engage in a conversation. And so we are left with a choice. We can either spiral down into cynicism or, worse, deny the Preacher's words altogether and continue to tensely pursue pleasures, intellect, and success, believing they will bring us happiness for all eternity. Or, knowing that everything is fleeting, we can relax; we can let go, we can be at ease. We can enjoy simple, divine, and earthy gifts in the present. We can trust in God's sovereignty. Here, hevel is not something to fear but a soothing balm that lifts the world's weight off our shoulders. We can just be. The choice is ours.

REFLECT

PAUSE Sit up straight.
Take a deep breath.
Reading the verses today, take a moment to reflect on the story.

PONDER Invite God to speak to you

I. What in your life would the Preacher call *hevel*? Do you agree?
II. Is there a time when you pursued something with all your might, only to find it futile? How did you respond to that futility?

PRAYER

Righteous and wise God, help me to pursue
only the excellent and everlasting
and let the futile dissipate from my desires.
Show me how to be present with you. Amen.

ASSIGNMENT: Please read John 4:28-29 for Lesson Twenty-Six.

CHAPTER
26

THE STORY OF THE SAMARITAN WOMAN AT THE WELL

Alienation / Belonging
John 4:28-29

LESSON TWENTY-SIX

SYNOPSIS An outcast, an alienated woman, goes alone to a drinking well for water and finds Jesus, who offers her much more than she could ever expect—belonging.

Read When Jesus chooses to journey through Samaria, he enters a region fraught with tense interethnic history. His Jewish people and the people of Samaria are not on friendly terms. They are alienated from one another.

As Jesus sends his disciples off into town and sits down to rest at Jacob's well alone, he may have been surprised to see a Samaritan woman approach the well alone.

The other women from her town may have walked to the well together earlier in the morning, chatting. They may have sometimes talked about her. What was that one woman's deal, that she had had five different husbands? Perhaps this woman's noontime solo journeys to draw water are daily reminders of her alienation from her community.

Likely, people in her village made assumptions about her character that may or may not have been confirmed. In a world where women were not allowed to initiate divorce, surely this woman's marital history says more about her husbands than about her. But she is alone, nonetheless.

If Jesus is surprised to see her, she must have been even more surprised to see him, mainly to hear him speak to her. "Give me a drink," he says, initiating conversation. But she knows Jews do not associate with Samaritans, and she knows he must know that as well.

The Jewish and Samaritan people shared a common history, ancestor, Jacob, and belief in a coming Messiah. Yet, these two groups avoided one another. They worshiped in different places—one group in Jerusalem, the other on the mountain where their ancestors worshiped.

Despite this interethnic alienation, Jesus makes himself clear: His offer of living water is for everyone. It is not limited to his own ethnic or religious group. His offer is for Samaritans, especially Samaritan women who are social outcasts even among their people. Everyone belongs.

Jesus' living water is for the lonely and isolated. It's for people who don't have anyone to walk to the well and draw water with. It's for people who their communities have shamed.

Jesus' living water is water that satisfies. Those who drink it, he says, will never be thirsty again. It's water that—as the Greek word could be translated—*leaps up* or *gushes up* into eternal life. It's water that turns alienation into a healthy community and belonging. Water restores relationships that have turned sour or been broken—among individuals, like the Samaritan woman and the other women in her village, and even among whole communities, like the Jewish and Samaritan people.

By the end of the conversation, the Samaritan woman is no longer alone. She is invited to take her place among the true worshipers who worship God in spirit and truth—a group that includes people of every tribe, tongue, and nation, as the book of Revelation puts it. And now she returns to her village, no longer an outcast but a leader.

"Come and see," she says. And her whole village goes to meet Jesus for themselves.

TODAY In our modern world of smartphones and social media, there are more ways to connect with other people than ever before. And yet, many people are lonely. Many people feel isolated and alienated from those around them. We often find it challenging to be present face-to-face with friends and family—our phones are always at hand, a ready distraction. Many people want to connect with others but find meaningful relationships challenging to build and sustain.

And like the Samaritan woman, many of us might feel alienated from others within our communities. Perhaps we feel rejected by people we once trusted. We may not be responsible for the rejection, but in any case, we feel alone and companionless when others turn their backs.

Like the Jewish and Samaritan people in Jesus' day, we, too, experience divisions and disconnections among entire groups of people. For example, people of different religious denominations may worship in various spaces. We are often more ready to consider ourselves superior to others than to seek out connection in humility, openness, and learning, but this only leads to further isolation and detachment.

The discussion between the Samaritan woman and Jesus shows how a single conversation can change a person's or an entire group's experience from abandonment to togetherness. Jesus does not caveat or qualify the woman's belonging; instead, she already belongs simply because she is a child of God.

Brené Brown writes, "When you get to a place where you understand that love and belonging [...] is not something you have to earn, anything is possible." The woman's conversation with Jesus empowers her to believe she belongs, encouraging her to return to her community to share what she learned about Jesus. As a result, many people think.

As God's children, we are invited to have conversations like the one the Samaritan woman had with Jesus. We're asked to listen, understand, and celebrate our differences—and not to see those differences as reasons to alienate or shame ourselves or others. Instead, our invitation is to see others as deeply loved by God as God pulls us out of our alienation into communities of belonging.

REFLECT

PAUSE Sit up straight.
Take a deep breath.
Reading the verses today, take a moment to reflect on the story.

PONDER Invite God to speak to you

I. What is your experience with alienation? Have you ever felt alienated from the community or been on the other end, casting others away? Was belonging ever restored, and how?
II. What kinds of divisions between entire communities do you see in our world? How can you be a leader, like the Samaritan woman, and invite those communities to experience belonging?

PRAYER
God of the Well, would you fill us up
with more than what we came for.
Restore our belonging and mend our divisions
so that we may lead others to your living water. Amen.

ASSIGNMENT: Please read Acts Chapters 6 & 7 for Lesson Twenty-Seven.

THE STORY OF STEPHEN

Serving Present Needs
Acts 6-7

LESSON TWENTY-SEVEN

SYNOPSIS A servant of God and God's people, Stephen, rises to meet the needs of the most vulnerable in his community.

Read We begin in the middle of Jerusalem when the apostles' message of Jesus rapidly spreads across socio-economic divides. Though the apostles are just a handful of ministers, many pledge their belief in Jesus' way because of their teachings. Among those people is a Greek-speaking Jew full of faith—Stephen.

Stephen and his fellow believers gather regularly, and their collective daily needs begin to overwhelm the few apostles. A quarrel breaks out. Some of the Hellenistic (Greek-speaking) Jewish people raise against the Hebraic Jewish community leaders that their widows are being overlooked and left food insecure. The felt needs stall the apostles' efforts to preach the word to more people. Who will make sure there is food when they gather? Will there be enough distributed to everyone, even the most vulnerable?

The apostles propose that the people choose seven from amongst them who are full of the Spirit and Wisdom and appoint them to this responsibility. The community is pleased by this, and they move to appoint Stephen and six others to lead and tend to the needs of others. The word of God spreads even more rapidly.

Time passes in Jerusalem. Stephen serves day in and day out, helping the needs of people through wonders and miracles. Though many are in awe, rivalling sects fume and seek to end his efforts by attempting to debate and discredit him. Their efforts fail to stand against his authoritative words, making them boil even more. Getting more desperate, they persuade people to lie about Stephen's message. "[He] blaspheme[s] Moses and even God!"

The people, elders, and teachers of the law all get stirred up and seize Stephen to put him on trial before the high council. The high priest raises the accusations before Stephen. "Are these charges true?"

All eyes gaze at Stephen in anticipation; his face becomes supernaturally bright.

He scolds them with a monologue, emphasizing the stubbornness of their shared Jewish ancestors. From the generations of Abraham to Jacob, Moses, and David, their people have always turned away from God's promises and saving work. "Must you forever resist the Holy Spirit? That's what your ancestors did, and so do you! [. . .] You deliberately disobeyed God's law, even though you received it from the hands of angels."

A chaotic uproar ensues. Stephen sees this reaction, but full of God's Spirit, and turns his gaze from the violent scene to the heavens above.

"Look, I see heaven open and the Son of Man standing at the right hand of God."

Suddenly, in their anger, they all rush Stephen, drag him out of the city, and cast stones at him. As each stone strikes his body, he utters a prayer before his final breath. "Lord, do not hold this sin against them."

Stephen is buried, and many mourn his violent death. Within the same day, great persecution breaks out all over Jerusalem, and the Jewish believers in Jesus are scattered throughout Judea and Samaria.

TODAY Stephen had no idea what part he would play in God's unfolding work. His story, developing in the way it did, was novel and led to an inflection point for followers of Jesus. He's considered the first martyr of the church—a Greek-speaking Jew responsible for caring for the vulnerable.

Knowing the finitude and mortality of Stephen's life, we can glean a distinct thread woven throughout his story: service grounded in the present. Though he lacked clear foresight of where his life would go, he was always set on present needs—serving God and people. He heard the needs of the most vulnerable widows in his community and rose to the responsibility of helping make sure they were met. He saw those seeking (but yet to find) God and performed wonders and signs to help them believe. He received the brutality unleashed by his accusers but returned compassion towards their violence and petitioned God for the forgiveness they needed.

So often in our modern world, we are fixated on the future and, as a result, disconnected from what we can do today. But, like Stephen, we don't know what will happen to us tomorrow. We can, instead, live with a focus on serving the present needs in our world. Theologian Henri Nouwen describes this present serving, "Our humanity comes to its fullest bloom in giving. We become beautiful when we give whatever we can: a smile, a handshake, a kiss, an embrace, a word of love, a present, a part of our life…all of our life."

How can our actions reflect the exact value of serving others *today*? When we look around right now, who do we see in need? Like Stephen, we may never see the complete realization of our services to the world, but by accepting this reality, we permit ourselves to be *fully* human—finite and beautiful. Here, we embrace our fragility and release to an eternal God our plans for tomorrow. God's cosmic work is constantly unfolding, and we are invited to serve here and now in this generation.

MORE THAN WORDS

REFLECT
PAUSE Sit up straight.
Take a deep breath.
Reading the verses today, take a moment to reflect on the story.
PONDER Invite God to speak to you

I. Where do we see the needs that the world presents to us today? What can we do to be more like Stephen, rising to meet physical and spiritual needs?
II. Are there moments in your life's story in which your actions to meet present needs have ultimately connected to God's eternal healing work?

PRAYER
God over all needs; please help me see as you see
and open my eyes to present needs.
Please grant me the resolve to serve the vulnerable
and those persecuting me. Only if you know the eternal story fully
will I be fully human. Amen.

ASSIGNMENT: Please read Genesis 38 for Lesson Twenty-Eight.

THE STORY OF TAMAR

God's Surprising Care & Justice
Genesis 38

LESSON TWENTY-EIGHT

SYNOPSIS Tamar is caught in a cycle of tragedy and neglect, but she takes a risk to ensure justice for herself and ultimately writes her great legacy.

Read Tamar is a Hebrew woman who marries Er, Judah's oldest son, one of Joseph's brothers. We don't know much about Er except that he is unjust and immoral in the eyes of God, and so he dies. As is customary, Judah has his next oldest son, Onan, marry Tamar as a surrogate. But because Onan knows that any child, he has with Tamar would be his brother's, he refuses to get her pregnant. God considers this unjust and immoral, so Onan also dies.

Judah has now lost two sons also die. Thinking of his son alone, Judah sends Tamar back to her father's household to live as a widow until Shelah has grown up. Judah has no intention of letting Tamar marry Shelah, but maybe this lie could buy him some time.

This is where the story gets interesting. Tamar is brilliant; she knows the injustice Judah is doing to her. Without children or a husband, she would have no promise of protection after her father and father-in-law died. Tamar certainly could have sat back and accepted her situation; no one would have blamed her. But instead, in the face of Judah's failure to protect her, she takes a huge risk to defend herself. After all, what did she have to lose?

Tamar hears Judah would be going through her area to shear his sheep. Jumping at the opportunity, Tamar disguises herself with a veil and waits along the road. Sure enough, as Judah passes by, he doesn't recognize her. Instead, he propositions her, promising to send her a sheep later as payment. Seeing another opportunity, Tamar accepts and requests that as collateral, he gives her his seal, cord, and staff—also forms of his identification.

Time passes and word spreads that Judah's widowed daughter-in-law is pregnant, the father unknown. This is an offense punishable by death and Judah sees an opportunity to be rid of Tamar once and for all. He sends for her to be brought out and burned.

Facing death, Tamar makes one final bid for her future. She sends Judah the cord, staff, and seal with a message: "I'm pregnant by the man who owns these." Judah is called out in front of the community, and he cannot deny what he has done. Instead, Judah confesses that he is in the wrong, not Tamar. He even acknowledges that she is more just, more righteous, than he is. He lets Tamar live, and he leaves her alone.

But the most striking part of all? The first of the twins Tamar gave birth to is Perez, an ancestor of David found in the genealogy of Jesus alongside his mother, one of only four women acknowledged. All along, Tamar's future is protected by God, and her legacy is far more incredible than she could have ever imagined.

TODAY What can we learn from Tamar's story today? Many of us will unlikely find ourselves in the same situation as Tamar. But we, too, may find ourselves in situations where we feel powerless or hopeless.

Tamar may have initially felt like she had no options, but God was with her, advocating for her. God saw the injustice done to Tamar in her first two marriages and by Judah and protected her. Tamar isn't a passive participant in the story. Instead, she is brave and takes an acute risk. We may think she is cunning or conniving when reading the story. Should we judge Tamar for her deceptiveness? Does God? Looking deeper at the story that unfolds, we catch a glimpse of what God values and who God is.

God cares about injustices placed on those most on the margins of society—in this case, a childless widow. Rather than seeing deception, God sees Tamar's intelligence and bravery, so much so that Judah publicly acknowledges she is more just and righteous than he. Ultimately, her story is woven into the beautiful story of salvation, being part of Jesus' genealogy.

From Tamar, we can learn to trust God to see our challenges and the injustices done to us and that God cares. We can learn to trust that God advocates for us even without an advocate. Even amidst the messiness of our lives, God is there, and like Tamar, we can act bravely and cunningly on our behalf, trusting God's caring justice is there, empowering us all along.

REFLECT

PAUSE Sit up straight.
Take a deep breath.
Reading the verses today, take a moment to reflect on the story.

PONDER Invite God to speak to you

I. How do we feel as we hear the events of Tamar's story? How can we learn to mourn the brokenness of cycles that keep people victims of their circumstances? How can we gain compassion for those seeking justice in an unjust world?
II. Do you find yourself feeling hopeless or powerless in the face of certain situations? How might God empower you to seek care and justice for yourself and others? How is God present in your challenges?

PRAYER

Sovereign God, we know that you see
the reality of our broken world
and care for victims seeking justice.
We pray that you will empower us
to make a way for ourselves against oppression. Amen.

ASSIGNMENT: Please read Proverbs 1:20-33 for Lesson Twenty-Nine.

THE STORY OF WISDOM

Relationship With Wisdom
Proverbs 1:20-33

LESSON TWENTY-NINE

SYNOPSIS   Wisdom is personified as a woman calling out to those who will listen. She warns of the tragedy in wait for those who reject her.

Read   Imagine yourself as an ancient Israelite. You walk through the dusty marketplace, filling your basket with wheat loaves for tonight's dinner. A choir of donkeys bray in the streets, and sellers try to make themselves heard over the pack animal voices. The soft chink of silver coins drawn from purses adds some snare to the bazaar symphony.

Then, you hear a new voice. It's coming from the public square, a dozen paces past the stalls. A woman's voice rings clear against the chaos of the marketplace haggling. This woman speaks with authority. She wants everyone to hear. She demands attention in such a way that you must choose: listen to her or ignore her.

What will you do?

The Book of Proverbs is a collection of sayings, likely compiled to train young men in the royal courts. Its overarching theme is learning wisdom by listening to the lived experiences of those who have gone before us.

This first chapter introduces us to a beautiful character. Her name is Wisdom. She is the poetic personification of God's wisdom. In chapter one, she is portrayed as a woman calling out in the streets. She makes her address in a very public place, where the city leaders typically hold court.

In verse 23, we get a snapshot of her heart. She longs to bare her soul to those who will listen and share the universe's secrets with those who heed her advice.

The verses following are her warnings. She invites us to meditate on how destructive it is to shun wisdom. The poetic imagery is that of building a relationship. The foolish build relationships with her only when they are desperate, and they ignore her when they don't quickly understand her benefits.

Wisdom feels this.

She feels the pain of being turned to only when situations are dire. She is not naïve. She understands the manipulative ways people try to take advantage of her resources without genuinely caring for her. Wisdom hates this. She is hurt when people try to use her only when it's convenient for them. She asks us to listen to her even when life is going well—when her words don't make a big difference. Just as we ought not to seek our friends' company only when in good spirits, we should not seek wisdom only in times of disaster. In verse 26, we see the harsh image of wisdom laughing at fools' destruction.3 This is the reality of our universe. Wisdom does not work when practiced at the last minute.

If we wait too long to build our relationship with her, even God's divine Wisdom will not prevent our self-imposed destruction.

In the last verse of the chapter, we see Wisdom's compassion yet again. She reaches out with a warm embrace to anyone who would build a relationship with her. She offers deep peace to those who would choose to speak with her.

Wisdom teaches us how to approach the rest of the Book of Proverbs. In this book, we may find advice that sounds good but is only sometimes necessary, such as sayings that encourage us to be diligent or listen to our elders. While we may not need to put that Proverb into practice now, how we interact with it builds our relationship with Wisdom. This applies not simply to the Book of Proverbs but stands for all the wisdom we find throughout life. Wisdom is calling to us. She wants to speak.

TODAY Take some time to meditate on the metaphor of Wisdom as a woman who wants to have conversations with us. This sharply contrasts how our academic system has taught us to read most scientific or historical nonfiction. Proverbs introduces this character to show that wisdom is not an intellectual resource. We bank up to pull out an encouraging one-liner when we need help. Instead, wisdom should be talked to and consulted with, like a caring mother who wants the best for us.

In our world, this picture of wisdom could be better for business. Much of our economy thrives from people wanting the low-effort, mindless, most pleasurable solution to everything. But this is the scheme of folly—bombarding us with quick-fix platitudes and promises to get us to want, need, and buy more things. These messages feel good to hear, but we know something more profound that can fulfill us. We already hear Wisdom's voice. Calling out to us. Yet amidst the bombarding messages, it is so easy to ignore her.

Then, at the brink of breakdown, we might ask God for advice. This conditional affair breaks Wisdom's heart. Why wait so long before speaking with Wisdom, who has been calling for us this whole time?

The invitation of Proverbs 1:20-33 is to practice wisdom even amidst the little things. Wisdom, just like a relationship, is something that takes effort and practice. Take a moment and think of some wisdom that may be useful in life. Consider moments of screen time or media consumption in the past week. Consider our relationships—with friends, family, and the earth. Are we in regular conversation with Wisdom about these things and more? In everything, Wisdom calls out to us, it is our choice to listen.

REFLECT
PAUSE   Sit up straight.
                   Take a deep breath.
                   Reading the verses today, take a moment to reflect on the story.
PONDER   Invite God to speak to you

I. What makes it hard to listen to wisdom?
II. How has wisdom led you to safety and ease?
III. Think of one practical wisdom you can implement this week. Use it to grow your relationship with Wisdom.

PRAYER
Heavenly Father, I want your wisdom
to permeate every aspect of my life.
Help me hear Wisdom's call and deliver me
from all the voices encouraging me to live foolishly.
I want to live a thriving life and learn to interact with the universe
as you intended. Bless me with your wisdom. Amen.

ASSIGNMENT: Please read Mark 14:1-9 for Lesson Thirty.

THE STORY OF THE WOMAN WHO ANOINTS JESUS

Generosity / Beauty
Mark 14:1-9

LESSON THIRTY

SYNOPSIS A woman breaks an alabaster jar of perfume onto Jesus' head; to the others in the room, it is wasteful and foolish; to Jesus, it is generous and beautiful.

Read The story begins with the chief priests and teachers of the law secretly plotting to arrest and kill Jesus. They have had enough of this so-called Messiah and are ready to put an end to him.

Jesus, meanwhile, reclines at Simon the Leper's table. Suddenly, an unnamed woman enters the home. Eyes dart towards her as she pulls out an alabaster jar of expensive perfume—worth an entire year's wages. She breaks it and pours it all over Jesus' head. His hair soaks in liquid as the fragrance fills the room.

The woman's startling act shakes everyone. Many in the room become resentful and indignant and talk down to her. "Why this waste of perfume? It could have been sold for more than a year's wages and the money given to the poor."

Historically, jars of perfume were intended as dowry gifts. So, there she is, an unnamed woman, not only giving up her potential for a future marriage and security but receiving the full blunt force of mockery and disgust. All gazes are upon her. She is exposed and alone.

Yet, despite experiencing all of this dismay, the woman chooses to act. She knows her status as an unmarried woman, and she knows she is breaking every cultural norm, but she breaks the jar anyway. It is a moment of courage.

Upon hearing the deafening insults of the crowd, Jesus steps in and defends the woman. "Leave her alone. Why are you bothering her? She has done a beautiful thing to me. The woman's act is immediately validated. Jesus, aware of his impending death, sees the woman's actions as preparation for his burial. She did what she could." In Jesus' eyes, the woman is seen as *generous instead of wasteful.* The woman sees Jesus as worth *everything.* She holds nothing back and generously gives, quite literally, all that she has to Jesus.

Instead of being unruly or unjustifiable, the woman's act is seen as beautiful. Translated as kalos in the original Greek, Jesus sees the woman's act as more than just an aesthetic decision; it is imbued with goodness, virtue, ethics, and morality.

Jesus continues by asserting that women's actions will be declared worldwide. This single act, he says, will reverberate throughout history wherever the gospel is preached. The woman's story begins in a place of exposure, being seen as disturbing and foolish—it ends with her story being seen as worth sharing as a model of generosity and beauty for generations to come.

TODAY Looking at the story of this unnamed woman, we see what generosity looks like. While the others in the room saw the woman's actions as inherently wasteful since they could have been given to the poor, the woman understands true generosity: an overflow of our loving relationship with God and Creation. Giving is good, but when we deduce charity or altruism to merely a transaction or practicalities—like the others in the room—we lose out on the complete picture of generosity.

The woman's story invites us to consider where our acts of generosity stem from. Do we give because we feel obligated, shamed, or forced? Is generosity another thing to do on our "good" human behavior checklist? Or, worse, do we give because it "looks good," choosing to virtue signal but not giving in good faith?

Instead, the woman's story asks us to give because of something more profound—a kinship with others, a love for God, a desire for all creation to thrive. When we give from these places, it might look funny, awkward, or troubling to others. It might subvert expectations; we might even be judged. But Jesus sees these acts for what they are: entirely, wholly generous.

Jesus shows the woman and the people in the room that generosity is more than simply a "nice thing." It is beautiful. In the original Greek, generosity is kalos, an outward sign of inward goodness. When we act like the unnamed woman, we participate in something holy and beautiful.

Reflecting on our lives today, we are invited to bend towards generosity, knowing God is generous with us. Like the woman, a single action of kindness might echo throughout the world, throughout history, for generations after us.

REFLECT

PAUSE Sit up straight.
Take a deep breath.
Reading the verses today, take a moment to reflect on the story.

PONDER Invite God to speak to you

I. When was the last time someone was generous with you? What did it look, sound, smell, taste, and/or feel like?
II. Where can you be generous?
III. Where does your generosity stem from? How can it be more beautiful?

PRAYER

God of beauty, thank you for all of who you are.
Teach me the fullness of generosity.
Please show me where I can participate in your generous spirit.
Help me see *kalos* all around me. Amen.

CONGRATULATIONS!!!
Your commitment to finish the course will undoubtedly encourage others
to know more about the Bible,
because it is MORE THAN WORDS.
It's alive!!!
God bless you always.

Danny Ninal has a Bachelor's Degree in Philosophy and English from San Carlos Seminary College, Cebu City, Philippines. His interests include Christian History, Philosophy, Law, Systematic Theology, Classical and Modern Literature, Poetry, Economics, Politics, Business Management, Information Technology Systems, and Music. All these converge into one potent writing machine which puts into the written word a juxta-position of profound messages beautifully intertwined with compelling storylines. Danny is currently the Lead Pastor of World Harvest Fellowship – Auckland. He lives in Auckland City, New Zealand, with his wife, Jia, and his only daughter, Danielle Angelika.

Printed by Libri Plureos GmbH in Hamburg, Germany